Stock Options Work ½ Hour a Day

Harsimran Singh, Ph.D.

ੴ

Unfortunately, this book does not cover "Dr. Singh's 3 & 4 legged strategies" as they were discovered after the book was printed. Visit our website and attend a webinar conducted by Dr. Singh. www.StockMarketExpert.com

Table of Contents

Chapter 10

Chapter 11

Dedication

Dedicated to my family, Satnam, Punit, Gunit and Pavit, who for so many years went up and down with me emotionally as the Down Jones Industrial Average went up and down financially. But all the while they were patient, and I am grateful beyond words for them, because my family's patience taught me patience of my own. As a result, I am now able to trade for a mere 15 minutes a day so peacefully as if this is my meditation time. In the following pages, I hope to teach the same to you.

Preface

Work ½ Hour a day!
(I actually work 15 minutes a day!!)

Writing a book on stock options was an accident. It was an accident somewhat similar to what prompted me to write books on *The Power of Prayer* and *Interfaith Religions*. It was the practical experience of power of prayer that made me write those books.

Not long ago, I met a gentleman who taught options for 20 years. He suggested that I do certain things in the market which led me to lot of disappointments. Not that he meant any harm, but his teachings lacked practical knowledge. I have read works by many authors on stocks and options. I found the same problem in most of them; they talked theoretical knowledge but lacked practical experience. In most instances it was like a swimming instructor teaching someone how to swim without ever entering a pool.

I was therefore prompted to write down my practical experiences, and that took the shape of the book in your hand. You may have come across many books which have very exciting titles, and state that you will make millions working only a few hours a day. They never sum up their ideas in any kind of practical training, enabling readers to make money in a certain way. They get the readers excited emotionally, without giving them any practical direction.

This book is different.

It is the gist of my experiences, which did not come easy for me. I learned by trading more than $100 million in my account. Learn from me. It is cheaper to borrow experience than to buy it. In this case, you are paying only the cost of the book to learn, what cost me millions to learn.

I have rejected many strategies mostly used by traders, and summed up only a couple of them which I believe seem good in the chapter “The Best Strategies”. All you have to do is to outsource the work of preparing a spread sheet on a daily basis, and see if any of options meet your criteria outlined in these strategies. In my case, I had outsourced this work to someone in India. Because of the time difference, I had the spread sheets on my screen before I began my day each morning. He even marked the options in bold and different colors according to my criteria, so it did not take me more than 5 minutes to find the best.

Until and unless you develop a system to work less than a ½ hour a day on trading options, it is very hard to make money in options trading. If you work too hard and too many hours, you simply fall in line with the majority of traders who make money today only to lose much more tomorrow or the day after.

I wish you luck in trading options.

Acknowledgments

Author is thankful to Mr. Surendar Vaddepali for helping me giving final touches to the book in many different ways.

Author is extremely grateful to Mr. Ernie Zerenner, President of Power Financial Group, Inc. for allowing the use of copy and texts from the PowerOptions Web site at http://www.poweropt.com.

Since 1997, PowerOptions has developed a set of online software tools to support options traders. Some of these tools are patented and copyrighted. Access to written copy and graphics is provided for educational and informative purposes only. The Author is not affiliated with, sponsoring, sponsored by, endorsing or endorsed by PowerOptions. No information presented by the author has been approved or endorsed by PowerOptions and does not constitute a recommendation by PowerOptions to buy or sell a particular security or investment strategy. Readers are solely responsible for their investment decisions. Both author and PowerOptions make no investment recommendations and do not provide any financial, tax, or legal advice. Please consult your tax consultant or financial advisor prior to making any investment.

Author is also very thankful to Mr. Charles Mellilo, a securities industry professional, and Director of Operations for PNiGlobal Partners, for reviewing this book in its entirety. His suggestions were extremely helpful.

Self-Discipline—The Tool to success

On a day to day basis, the stock market is governed predominantly by greed and fear. This is evidenced by the market going up hundreds of points on one day, and falling hundreds of points on the next day. Sometimes that sort of volatility is seen on the same day. The so called market gurus, friends circle, other acquaintances and stock brokers can influence you in one way or the other. A stock broker may get someone excited with a phone call saying, the stock market is going up or going down. The fact is this statement is wrong to begin with. The stock broker should only be saying whether the stock market has gone up or down. No one can absolutely predict market movements. What prevents the market from reversing direction? Do as Warren Buffet does, invest in stocks for the long term. I have yet to meet any one who is a short term day trader in stocks, and has been able to retain earnings for a long period of time.

During the process of teaching you different strategies, I am bound to be wrong, not one time, but many times on a short term basis. The reason is very simple. Short term market movements tend to behave in a very illogical manner. The reason is fairly simple. On a short term basis market is governed by psychological forces. We have yet to come up with an instrument that can predict or measure human psychology. Hence, your wrong strategies are bound to be right many times. Once you have made money utilizing one of these strategies, you become victim to your own wrong doings. At one time or another, you end up losing all your gains and more.

The hardest part in this game of trading is to kill your ego. Your ego is the biggest negative force which may lead to disasters. Before placing an order for a trade, you have to convince yourself that the market may lead your stock in the opposite direction and you don't know the direction of the market. You are bound to be right at some time or another. Once you are right, you tend to forget the number of times you were wrong. This is simply human nature and it is difficult to fight against it.

Be greedy. Buy when most people are selling. Also, be fearful. Sell when most people are buying. I do not mean that you always buy when market is falling down or sell when market it when market is going up. You must still stick to your fundament principles of trading. Your moods and daily life should not be governed by the graphs of Dow Jones.

Trust me, if you don't have self-discipline, don't trade in the stock market. You are better off not reading another page of this book. Have fun in a casino and satisfy your gambling instincts there. Losing in casinos may be much cheaper than losing your hard earned savings in the stock market.

I know it is easier said than done, but you have to develop self-discipline whereby you control your greed and fear. I have made an attempt to teach self-discipline in my book, "26 Steps To Spiritual and Financial Riches - How Spirituality Led to a $7 million gain." I am of firm belief that all my teachings will be in vain without self-discipline. I am therefore offering this book for free to all my readers. You can down load this book free from our website www.BillionaireBestSellers.com. If you want a hard copy of the book, please write to us at P O Box 570, Oyster Bay, NY 11771.

Chapter 1

Overview of Options Trading

History of Options Trading

It is believed that options have been started in ancient times and were used in trading agriculture commodities. Options in stocks started when trading took place in stocks. However, they were not as popular as stocks due to insufficient marketing. It was difficult to find option sellers, even though buyers were there. Option trading officially began when the Chicago Board of Trade (CBOT) came into existence, in 1848. Other exchanges such as the Minneapolis Grain Exchange, Kansas City Board of Trade and New York Cotton Exchange came into existence later on. However, option trading did not become popular. The total annual trading volume of options was below 300,000 contracts until the mid-twentieth century, when the volume reached 200,000 contracts per day in the 1970s. This was a result of the 1968 formation of the Chicago Board Options Exchange (CBOE). This has facilitated liquidity for options. Initially, the CBOE was set up just for call option trading. In the later 70s put options had gained in importance, and they began to trade as well. SPX started index options on the CBOE. Having seen an increase in the popularity of options trading, other exchanges such as the NYSE and NASDAQ also started stock option trading in 1985.

Types of Options

Warrant, call option and put option are the options exist in options trading.

A **Warrant** is an instrument issued by a firm, which gives right to the holder to buy stocks from the firm at a particular price during a designated period. The life of warrants typically has a longer time frame than options. Companies or brokerage houses can issue warrants and they tend to have limited liquidity in the secondary market.

Options exchanges create options and are issued generally by other investors. Buying or selling of options mean that one need not buy or sell them to exercise them physically but are used as tool to manage risk. The price of an option is quoted per share basis but they are usually sold in a lot of one-hundred shares or in multiple of one-hundred. Occasionally, options will trade in contracts other than one-hundred shares, or with cash. This is as a result of a stock or cash dividend issued on the underlying security.

A call option is an instrument that is generally issued by a trader. The buyer gets right to purchase the underlying asset at an agreed price (also called as strike price) within the agreed period or before expiration date. You would purchase a call option when you expect the underlying stock price to go up before the expiration date. The call option buyers are only risking the amount of money used to purchase the option; therefore, they are exposed to limited risk if the market goes down. In theory, a stock can always go higher. The purchaser of the call has unlimited profit potential.

A put option is an instrument that gives the purchaser the right to sell a stock at a specified price (also called as strike price) before the expiration date of the contract. You would purchase a put option when you expect the price to go down prior to the expiration date. Put option buyers are also exposed to limited risk because they are only risking the amount paid for the option. However, they also have limited profit potential, because a security can only go to zero.

Strike Price

A strike price is a specified price at which a transaction in the underlying stock is exercised. This is the agreed price to buy, in the case of a call option, or to sell, in the case of a put option, when the option is exercised prior to its expiration date. An option contract's strike price is expressed on a per share basis. This means a strike price of 25 would mean $25 per share. An option's strike price does not change, and is unaffected by the current market price of the underlying stock. The strike price difference generally ranges 2.5 to 5. The difference between the strike price and the premium paid or received on the option contract will determine the profit or loss on the option contract.

Option Premium

The option premium is the cost to acquire the option. There are two components of the option premium, time value and intrinsic value. The time value component is the amount of premium paid for the amount of time remaining until expiration of the option. The more time until expiration, the greater the time value. The intrinsic value is the "in the money" difference between the strike price and the current market price. For example, if a call option has a strike price of $25, and the current price is $30, then it will have five points, or dollars, of intrinsic value per share in the premium. If an option is out of the money, meaning that the strike price of the option is less favorable than the current market price, it has no intrinsic value.

Expiration Date

Expiration date is the day on which option is exercised. It is the day on which value of option gets terminated and it becomes worthless if it is not exercised. This date is generally mentioned at the time of writing an option to include the month and date. A European option shall be exercised only on the expiration date whereas an American option can be exercised any trading day prior to expiration. This day is usually the third Friday of the contract expiration month. The expiration day will be prior to Friday if the third Friday happens to be a holiday.

A contract, particularly whose value is out-of-money (OTM), may not be exercised as it does not give any profit for the trader on the expiration date. It becomes valueless in such cases.

Settlement Date

The settlement date is exactly what the name would imply. It is the date that the transaction is settled, or paid for. Unlike settlement for a stock transaction, which occurs in three business days, option transactions settle on the next business day.

Simply put, when you purchase an option, the cost of the transaction must available in your brokerage account on the very next business day. Also, it is important to remember that although options may be purchased in a margin account, they must still be paid for in full.

Call Options

Call options are derivatives which establish a contractual relationship between a holder and a writer of an option contract. The holder of call option gets the right, but not obligation, to own the underlying stock at the strike price before the option expires. When you buy a call option, it means that you buy a right to purchase shares at a particular strike price before its expiration date. The seller (also called the writer) of the call option, however, has to deliver the underlying stock when option is exercised. Call options will be available in different strike prices depending upon the market price of the underlying asset. The premium of the call option would be debited from your account, and becomes your maximum loss if the option is not exercised. You incur this loss when the price of the stock trades below the strike price. You realize a profit if the market price of underlying assets trades above the strike price before expiration date. The higher the price above the strike price, the higher the value addition to the profits.

	Holder (Buyer)	**Writer (Seller)**
Call Option	Right to Buy	Obligation to sell

If you sell a call option that means that you sell a right to the buyer of the option to purchase the underlying stock at a specified price. You receive the option premium, which would be credited to your trading account. You retain the premium and it becomes your profit as long as the call option is not exercised before expiration date. If the option holder exercises the right to buy when the price of the underlying stock is above the strike price, then you as the seller must buy those shares at the prevailing market price and sell them at the agreed strike price. This situation creates a potential loss to the writer of the contract. The writer, or seller, is exposed to unlimited loss potential. With respect to the holder of a call option, it is important to remember the following:

- If the Strike price is equal to Stock Price is said to be at-the-money (ATM)
- If Strike price greater than stock price it is said to out-of-the-money (OTM)
- If the strike price less than stock price, it is said to be in-the-money (ITM)

With respect to a holder of a put option, the reverse is true.

Example

InterMune Inc. (ITMN) stock closed at $11.09 on November 14th, 2008. If you buy one April 2009 call option with a strike price of $10, you will get the right to buy ITMN stock at $10 per share prior to April 2009, by paying a premium of $6.40 per share.

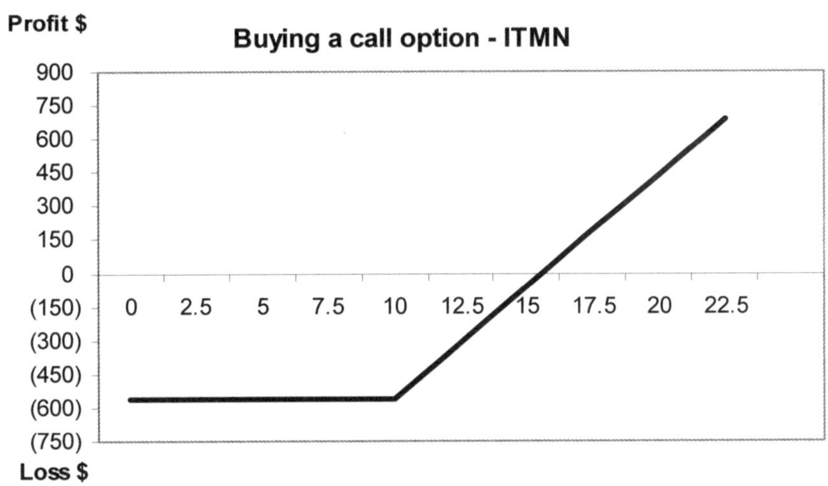

You will profit if the price of ITMN goes above $16.40 ($10.00 + $6.40) before the expiration date. If the stock closes below $10 on expiration date, you wouldn't exercise your option and you forego your $6.40 per share whereby your maximum loss becomes $640 per option contract. You wouldn't be exercising your option if the price goes below the strike price.

If the price goes to $20 before expiration date, you would exercise your option to buy shares at $10, the strike price. Your net gain will be $3.60 per share when you account for the initial premium of $6.40 that you paid to acquire the right to buy stock at $10.

Example

If you have sold an April 2009 10 call option of ITMN at $6.40, you will profit if the price trades below the strike price plus the initial premium value as the buyer of the option would not exercise his option. The initial premium received of $640 will be your maximum profit. You will be exposed to losses if the price trades above $16.40.

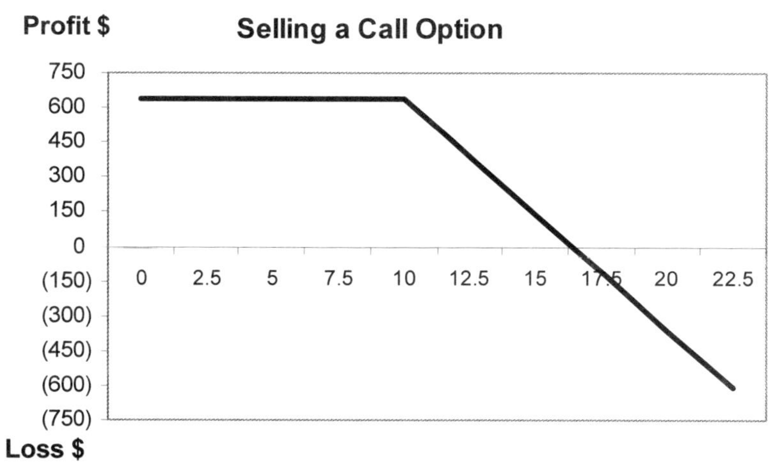

Put Options

Put options are derivatives which establishes a contractual relationship between the seller and the buyer of an option. The holder of an option agrees to buy the right to sell stock at a strike price before the expiration date. The buyer enjoys the option to sell the stock, but has no obligation to do so. The strike prices available in the market depend on the price of the stock.

You would buy (also termed as long) a put option when you expect the price of the stock to fall before expiration date. On the other hand, you would sell (also known as short) a put option when the market for that security is expected to be bullish, or increase, prior to the expiration date.

When you buy a put option, it means that you are buying a right to sell a specific stock at a specific, on or before a specific date. Your trading account will be debited the cost of buying the put option. You maximize your profit when the market becomes bearish and the price of the underlying security reaches $0.

People perceive buying or selling put options in different ways. Risk adverse people may buy a put option to protect a stock position in their portfolio from a drop in price. You can see increase in the option premium as the stock price decreases. You may choose to sell the option at the higher price. The resulting profit can then be utilized to offset the loss on the stock position.

	Holder (Buyer)	**Writer (Seller)**
Put Option	Right to Sell	Obligation to Buy

Let us take the ITMN example and see how buying put option makes profit or losses. The premium for buying an April 2009 10 put option is $5 per share. The chart below shows the scenario.

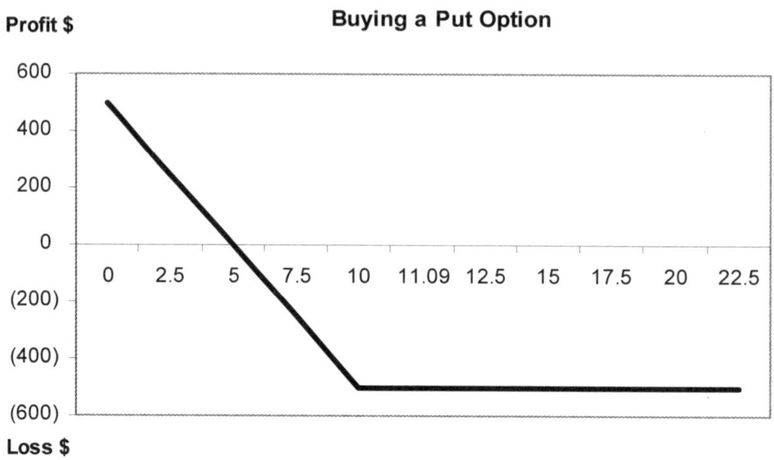

As the price of the underlying stock decreases, the profit potential continues to increase. Your maximum profit is realized if the stock price reaches $0. The maximum loss however is limited to $500. This is because that the holder does not want to exercise his option if the market value is greater than the strike price. The holder will only exercise his right when the stock goes down below the strike price, which results in a profit.

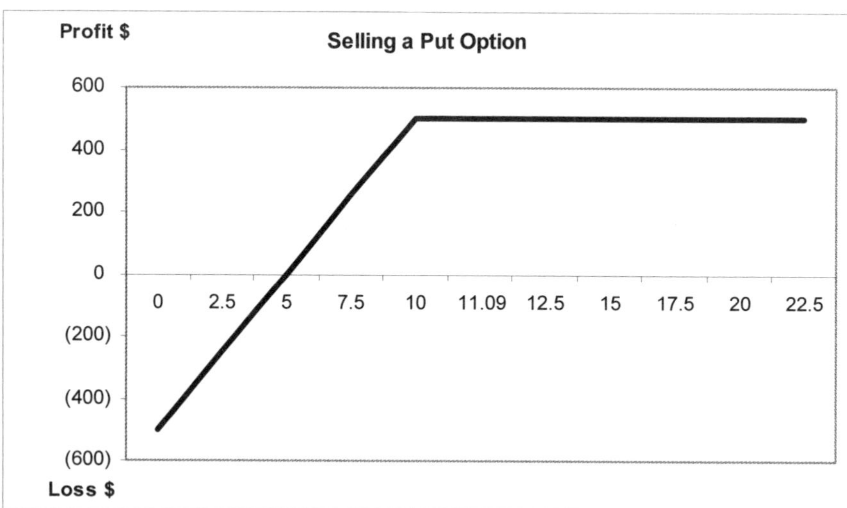

If you choose to sell a put option, the reverse will apply. The profit is limited to the amount of premium received when selling a put option. You enter into the "profit zone" when the stock price trades above $5. If the stock is trading at $10 or above on expiration date, you make a profit of $500, which is your maximum profit.

Exercise of Options

Exercise here means that the holder of the option is invocating his/her right in accordance with the rules and regulations framed by the Options Clearing Corporation (OCC). Option holders can exercise his right to buy or sell shares throughout the life of the option contract. The seller of the option is always obligated to fulfill their obligation whenever the seller is assigned an exercised option contract. An option is deemed to be “assigned” when the seller of an option contract has been notified that the buyer has exercised his right. Before it is assigned, the seller may choose to close their position by "buying the option back". This means the seller has purchased an option contract identical to the one sold. The two positions offset each other, resulting in a "closed" position. Strike price is the key factor for options trading if transaction has to take place.

American exercise

In this style, the option can be exercised at any time before the expiration date. For example, you buy an April call option today; you may exercise your right any day before the expiration date. This style is widely used in options trading. The risk appetite is a little higher compared to European exercise as the holder assumes higher risk. The underlying stock can move in either direction and might be exposed to higher risk before expiration date. The key issue in this style of option is to watch the dividend payments during the life of the option. No dividend payments during the option life is considered to be a safe bet as it gives more intrinsic value for the option. If a dividend is paid, the seller of the call option "pays the dividend" on the contract in the same manner as is the investor were short the stock.

European exercise

This style of exercise is not popular from retail perspective. You may exercise your right only on the day of expiration. Options on S&P 500 stock index, NASDAQ index etc. fall under this style. The premium charged in this style of exercise will be lower as the holder has less risk and knows when this option can be exercised.

Why trade Options

Trading in options provides many benefits to both parties of an option. The buyer gets the right to buy or sell shares at a set price prior to a predetermined day. The seller has the potential benefit of generating income through the receipt of the option premium. It is pretty clear that trading in options is more complex and closer observation is required compared to trading stocks. However, the amount of risk sometimes can be better managed by both parties, allowing them to maximize their profits or to minimize their losses.

All the stocks do not have their options traded in exchanges. Options are generally available on large, well established companies. There may be some exceptions allowing a few smaller companies to have options traded. In order to qualify as an optionable stock, the following criteria need to be fulfilled:

- Stock shall be listed on an exchange
- Shareholders count shall exceed 2,000
- The company shall have over seven million publicly held shares
- There shall be minimum closing price in the past three months.

In spite of the educational efforts of the exchanges, there is still a misconception among investors that options trading is considered to be one of the risky investments, and are suitable for only the most experienced speculator. Although options do have significant risk, a wise and disciplined investor may profit from options trading, irrespective of the market price of the underlying stock going up, down or sideways. Success depends upon the ability of the trader to use the proper tools and analysis.

Traders generally enter into options trading in an effort to achieve any or all of the following objectives:

- To increase return on investment portfolio
- To get protection if the market goes against their expectations
- To buy or sell stock at a predetermined price at a later date
- To maximize returns irrespective of market being bullish or bearish

Apart from these, there are specific reasons why traders are attracted to trade in options.

1. Requires relatively small start-up capital

Trading in options require limited initial investment as compared to trading in stocks where full value of the share need to be invested. A trader can maximize profits or minimize losses by trading in options because they require only the premium, and not the full cost of the share price. One can have numerous option positions with the same amount of funds that would only secure one stock position.

2. Leverage

If you calculate the percentage of returns coming from a successful option trade, you would find that it is many times more than the returns generated from trading the actual stock. This is because the returns are generated using between five and ten percent of the investment required for stock trading. However, one should be very careful about the potential losses if a trade goes against expectations.

3. Hedging

Option trading allows investors to minimize their risk by adopting an appropriate strategy. Such a strategy will be used as hedge, in an effort to minimize losses. It can act as insurance from an unexpected price fluctuation of the underlying stock.

4. Flexibility

Using different strategies, option trading provides the opportunity to generate higher percentage returns on the money invested. One can have flexibility to use such strategies either to maximize profits or minimize losses.

5. Limited Risk

In many strategies, risk is limited to the extent of premium paid while entering into a trade. While this is true for the buyer of the option, it is not true for the seller of the option.

Though all of the above sounds quite good and may attract you to trade in options, the following are the drawbacks of options trading:

- Liquidity can be affected depending on the strike price of the option you buy or sell.
- There will be threat of time decay for the buyers of the options.
- The option positions need to be observed very closely.

In-The-Money, At-The-Money, and Out-Of-The-Money Options

Options fall in to three categories in the money, at the money, or out of the money. As the terms imply, it describes the price of the underlying stock relative to the strike price of the option.

	In-The-Money	At-The-Money	Out-Of-The-Money
Call	When current market price is > than the strike price	When current market price = the strike price	When current market price is < than the strike price
Put	When current market price is < than the strike price	When current market price = the strike price	When current market price is > than the strike price

In-The-Money

Call options are said to be "In-The-Money (ITM)" if the Strike Price is less than the current stock price and they are said to be "At-The-Money (ATM)" if the Strike Price is equal to the current stock price. An "Out-Of-The-Money" (OTM) call option is one whose strike price is above the stock price.

The option will have intrinsic value when a stock price is higher than the strike price in case of ITM. There will be no intrinsic value in case of OTM.

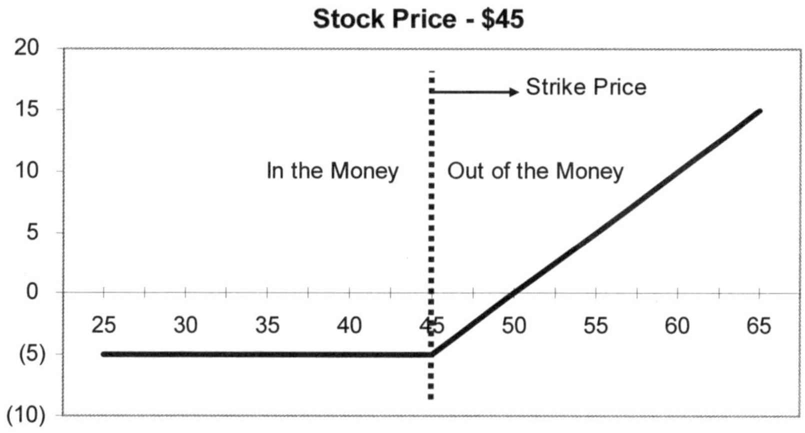

Call Option		
Stock Price	**Strike Price**	**Status**
$45	$35	**ITM**
$45	$40	**ITM**
$45	$45	**ATM**
$45	$50	**OTM**
$45	$55	**OTM**

Put options are just opposite of call options. If the stock price is less than strike price, the option is said to be in-the-money (ITM). It is said to be "At-The-Money

(ATM)" if the Strike Price is equal to the current stock price and it is ′out-of-the-money (OTM) if the stock price is more than the strike price.

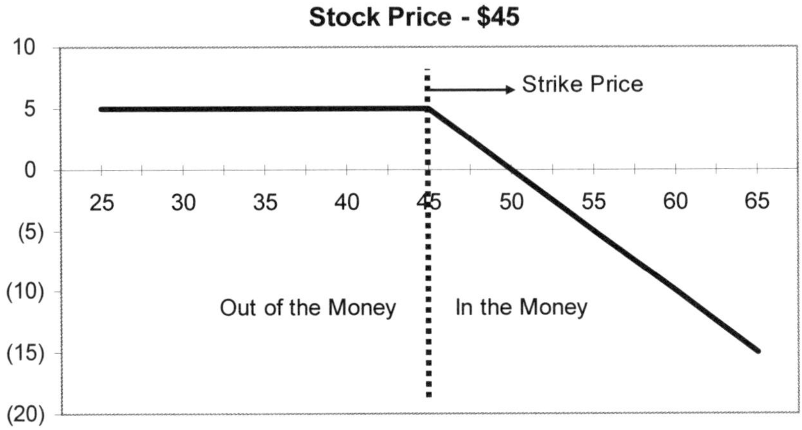

With the example given below, it becomes easy to understand.

Put Option		
Stock Price	**Strike Price**	**Status**
$45	$35	**OTM**
$45	$40	**OTM**
$45	$45	**ATM**
$45	$50	**ITM**
$45	$55	**ITM**

Option Price Components

An option's price is comprised of two components, intrinsic value and time value.

As outlined earlier, the Intrinsic Value is the "in the money" amount of the option premium. Intrinsic value tells us the value of the option if it is exercised immediately.

For example, if a stock is trading at $100 and its call has a strike price of $80, there is an intrinsic value of $20 per share. There will be no intrinsic value if the strike price of a call option is greater than its stock price.

Similarly for Put option, if the strike price is $125 and the stock price is at $100, there is an intrinsic value of $25 per share. There will be no intrinsic value if the strike price of put option is less than stock price.

Intrinsic value is calculated by subtracting the strike price from the price of the underlying (Underlying price - Strike price).

Time Value, also known as extrinsic value and premium value, is the difference between an option's price or premium, and its intrinsic value. It is determined based on the lifespan remaining and the volatility of the underlying stock. As the option nears expiration, the time value of the option decreases until it finally reaches zero. When the extrinsic value reaches zero, the option value will be equal only to its intrinsic value. The time value is dependent on time to expiration, interest rate, volatility and payment of dividends.

Time value equals the option premium minus the intrinsic value.

Example

Stock Price - $96	
Strike Price	Premium
90	10
95	6
100	3

Using the formulas; (Intrinsic value = Underlying stock price - Strike price), and (Time Value = Call Premium - Intrinsic Value), we would calculate those values of the option premium as follows:

At Strike Price of $90

$96 (underlying stock price) - $90 (strike price) = $6 (intrinsic value).

$10 (call Premium) - $6 (intrinsic value) = $4 (time value).

At Strike Price of $95

$96 (underlying stock price) - $95 (strike price) = $1 (intrinsic value).

$6 (call Premium) - $1 (intrinsic value) = $5 (time value).

At Strike Price of $100

$96 (underlying stock price) - $100 (strike price) = $-4 (intrinsic value).

If the calculation generates a negative number, or zero, there is no intrinsic value. Therefore, the entire option premium is comprised of time value.

$3 (call Premium) - $0 (intrinsic value) = $3 (time value).

The breakeven of a long call shall be equal to the sum of strike price and option premium. In this example the break even point for the 100 call is $103.

Stock Price - $96			
Strike Price	Premium	Intrinsic Value	Time Value
80	18	16	2
85	14	11	3
90	10	6	4
95	6	1	5
100	3	0	3

Potential Risk & Rewards of Options; Buyer vs. Seller

For the call option buyers, maximum loss is limited to the initial premium paid irrespective of the stock price, and profit potential is unlimited. For a put option buyer, the maximum loss is limited to the premium paid. However, because a stock can only go as low as zero, the maximum profit is limited to the strike price multiplied by the number of shares in the contract (usually one hundred), multiplied by the number of contracts.

The seller of the option contract, (the one who is obligated either to buy or sell stocks when the buyer exercises their right) tends to carry greater risk. Assuming that you do not already own the stock for which you are writing a call, you carry unlimited risk. This is because a stock, in theory, can always trade higher. Therefore, if you write a call that gets exercised, it is possible that you would have to purchase the share in the open market at whatever the current share price is, and deliver them at the strike price. Your maximum profit is limited to the premium you take in. There is limited profit potential with unlimited risk exposure when selling calls. Although selling puts does carry less risk than selling calls, it stills carries more risk than buying puts. This is because a stock could go to zero, but if you sold a put against that stock, you will likely end up paying the strike price for worthless securities.

	Profit	Loss
Buy Call	Unlimited	Limited to premium paid
Buy Put	Limited to: strike price x 100 x number of contracts	Limited to premium paid
Sell Call	Limited to premium received	Unlimited
Sell Put	Limited to premium received	Limited to: strike price x 100 x number of contracts

Hence buying options is preferable for new traders. As they gain experience, they can enter into other strategies that may minimize risk exposure and maximize profit potential simultaneously.

Option Chain

An option chain gives details of options of available at different strike prices. They show the symbols for each of the available strike prices along with details of stock price, month and expiration, bid price, ask price, last traded price, open interest etc. of the underlying security.

Understanding Symbols
The Stock Options names are written in the following manner: SYMBOL MP.

Symbol = the Option Root Symbol, or the symbol of the underlying security.
M = Expiration Month.
P = Strike Price.

An example of an option chain can be found on the following page.

View By Expiration: Dec 08 | **Jan 09** | Mar 09 | Jun 09 | Jan 10 | Jan 11

CALL OPTIONS

Strike	Symbol	Last	Chg	Bid	Ask	Vol	Open Int
12.5	HPAV.X	**12.3**	0	10.5	10.9	5	5
15	HPAC.X	**6.4**	0	8.2	8.6	100	111
17.5	HPAW.X	**5.4**	0	6	6.4	5	100
20	HPAD.X	**4.2**	↓ **0.4**	4.1	4.4	5	1,186
22.5	HPAX.X	**2.5**	0	2.6	2.8	1	312
25	HPAE.X	**1.6**	↑ **0.2**	1.45	1.6	16	1,164
30	HPAF.X	**0.4**	↑ **0.05**	0.3	0.4	37	711
35	HPAG.X	**0.2**	0	N/A	0.1	34	992
40	HPAH.X	**0.1**	0	N/A	0.05	3	1,311
45	HPAI.X	**0.05**	0	N/A	0.1	22	824
50	HPAJ.X	**0.05**	0	N/A	0.1	5	495
55	HPAK.X	**0.1**	0	N/A	0.1	2	983
60	HPAL.X	**0.15**	0	N/A	0.15	5	444
65	HPAM.X	**0.1**	0	N/A	0.15	7	642
70	HPAN.X	**0.1**	0	N/A	0.15	0	4,226
75	HPAO.X	**0.1**	0	N/A	0.15	3	2,072
80	HPAP.X	**0.2**	0	N/A	0.1	0	148
85	HPAQ.X	**0.1**	0	N/A	0.1	2	115
90	HPAR.X	**0.1**	0	N/A	0.1	0	66
95	HPAS.X	**0.05**	**0**	N/A	0.1	0	109
100	HPAT.X	**0.5**	0	N/A	0.1	0	41

PUT OPTIONS

Strike	Symbol	Last	Chg	Bid	Ask	Vol	Open Int
12.5	HPMV.X	**0.45**	0	0.05	0.15	253	276
15	HPMC.X	**0.2**	↓ **0.2**	0.2	0.25	26	596
17.5	HPMW.X	**0.65**	**0**	0.5	0.6	110	303
20	HPMD.X	**1.4**	0	1.05	1.15	7	800
22.5	HPMX.X	**2.45**	0	1.95	2.1	40	395
25	HPME.X	**3.4**	0	3.3	3.5	20	937
30	HPMF.X	**7.5**	0	7	7.3	10	832
35	HPMG.X	**9.4**	0	11.7	12.1	10	532
40	HPMH.X	**20**	0	16.6	17.1	10	276
45	HPMI.X	**22.48**	0	21.6	22.1	1	254
50	HPMJ.X	**24**	0	26.6	27.1	5	82
55	HPMK.X	**27.21**	**0**	31.6	32.2	20	44
60	HPML.X	**35.3**	0	36.7	37.2	0	10
65	HPMM.X	**16.57**	0	41.4	42.2	0	19
70	HPMN.X	**48**	0	46.4	47.1	20	150
75	HPMO.X	**51.8**	0	51.4	52.1	2	2

Microsoft	Jan 09 Call	$55
MQF	A	K
Expiration Month Codes		
Month	Call	Put
January	A	M
February	B	N
March	C	O
April	D	P
May	E	Q
June	F	R
July	G	S
August	H	T
September	I	U
October	J	V
November	K	W
December	L	X

Standard Strike Price Codes:

Code	Strike Prices						Code	Strike Prices					
A	5	105	205	305	405	505	N	70	170	270	370	470	570
B	10	110	210	310	410	510	O	75	175	275	375	475	575
C	15	115	215	315	415	515	P	80	180	280	380	480	580
D	20	120	220	320	420	520	Q	85	185	285	385	485	585
E	25	125	225	325	425	525	R	90	190	290	390	490	590
F	30	130	230	330	430	530	S	95	195	295	395	495	595
G	35	135	235	335	435	535	T	100	200	300	400	500	600
H	40	140	240	340	440	540	U	7.5	37.5	67.5	97.5	127.5	157.5
I	45	145	245	345	445	545	V	12.5	42.5	72.5	102.5	132.5	162.5
J	50	150	250	350	450	550	W	17.5	47.5	77.5	107.5	137.5	167.5
K	55	155	255	355	455	555	X	22.5	52.5	82.5	112.5	142.5	172.5
L	60	160	260	360	460	560	Y	27.5	57.5	87.5	117.5	147.5	177.5
M	65	165	265	365	465	565	Z	32.5	62.5	92.5	122.5	152.5	182.5

There are certain non-standard strike price codes. They can change at the discretion of Options Price Reporting Authority (OPRA) without prior notice.

How an Option is Priced

An investor would analyze how the options are priced before buying or selling an option within a particular time period. An investor should also understand what factors would affect an option's price when selecting an option.

The value of an option is determined by several factors relating to the underlying stock and the financial markets overall.

1. Option Strike Price

Strike price determines if an option is In-The-Money, At-The-Money, or Out-Of-The-Money. The value of calls decline when the strike price increases while it increases as the strike price declines. The reverse is true for puts.

2. Current Stock Price

Keeping all other factors constant, the option price of a call will go up and put will come down if price of the underlying stock is increased. It will be opposite when the price of stock decreases.

3. Time remaining until expiration

The longer the time period to expiration the more time value is created. The time value component of an option price erodes as its expiration date approaches. Due to time decay effect, an Out-Of-The-Money option price will decrease over time and finally expires worthless. Hence we can say it is an enemy of option buyers while it is a friend to option sellers. If you wish to make money in options trading in the long run, you should understand the impact of time on stock and option positions.

4. Implied Volatility

There will be uncertainty associated with the returns on investments made in options trading. Volatility is a measure of risk, or uncertainty, as to the movement of the price of the underlying stock. The higher the variance in the stock price, the greater the option value will be as there is a possibility that the options will end in your favor profitably. A good measure of a stock's volatility is its beta coefficient, or beta for short. A stock that has a beta of one, is deemed to be approximately as volatile as the market overall. A beta of two would signify that the stock is twice as volatile as the market, whereas a beta of less than one would signify a volatility less than that of the market. As a general rule, the more volatile a stock, the more time value created.

5. Interest Rate

Opportunity cost comes into the picture when the buyer purchases the option. This cost depends upon the level of interest rates and the number of days remaining until expiration of the option. The impact of interest rate is something described as the "carrying cost" of stocks. When you are bullish on a certain stock, it is good to buy a call option than the stock itself, as it requires less money.

Any change in the interest rate would affect stock prices. When interest rates increase, stock prices generally would fall as investors change their portfolio based on the risk levels. The value of calls generally will decrease and the value of puts generally will increase when there is an increase in interest rates.

6. Dividend

Any payment of a dividend during the period of an option contract would result in a decrease in the value of the stock. Hence, higher the cash dividends paid on a stock, lower will be the call premium and higher will be the put premium.

Option Volume and Open Interest

In stock trading, stock market activity and liquidity by volume are measured whereas in options trading Open Interest and Volume are measured.

Volume gives the market breadth, which indicates the market strength in the direction of the change. It can sometimes show reversal trends in the short term. A fixed number of shares are traded in options trading. Unlike in stock trading where there is a finite number of shares outstanding that can be traded, a new option can easily be created for trading. There wouldn't be any open interest when a new expiration month is initiated because there are no option contracts being traded for that month yet. As trading starts building up, open interest will also increase.

Now, what is Open Interest?

Open Interest tells us the number of options traded, but have not been liquidated, exercised, assigned, closed out, or allowed to expire. It represents the total number of option contracts that are held by market participants. This is used to confirm trends in futures and options contracts. It measures the amount of money entering into the market. Open interest is reported on daily basis representing changes in the size of option contract interest on each day.

An increase in the open interest represents flow of new money into the market while a decline represents outflow of money from the market which implies change in the trade. The summary of relationship between price and the open interest is summarized by the following table:

Price	Open Interest	Trend
Increase	Increase	Strong Market
Increase	Decrease	Weakening Market
Decrease	Increase	Strengthening Market
Decrease	Decrease	Weak Market

In order for open interest to increase, three things must happen. First and foremost, the option must exist. This means that if the option does not already exist, it must be created. Second, a purchaser of the option must create a long position (buy to open). Lastly, the seller of the option must be creating a new short position (sell to open). On the other hand, size of open interest decreases when options are closed out and, of course, when the contract does not exist. Open interest does not change simply because a new contract is created. It also does not change when a trader purchases an option to open, from a trader selling to close. The reason for this is simple. The seller of the option has now closed his position, and he no longer has a vested "interest" in the performance of the option. Had the trader sold to open (created a short position) he would then have an interest in the performance of the option.

An option can be closed by offsetting the transaction or by exercising it. One can offset a transaction if the buyer sells the option to close one's long position or if the seller purchases back the option to close a short position.

The difference between volume and open interest can be understood with the following example:

		Open Interest	Volume
Day1	No options were traded	0	0
Day2	X buys and Y sells 2 option contracts	2	2
Day3	A buys and B sells 8 option contracts	10	8
Day4	X closes his position and B closes partly by buying back 2 options	8	2
Day5	M buys 4 contracts from A	8	4

On day four, the open interest is reduced by two as X and B have their existing position already. This is an offsetting transaction to close out the position and hence two contracts disappear.

On day five, M buys four options from A. As a result, we find no change in the open interest as no new contracts were created. M replaces A, who wants to exit from his long position.

How to Determine Options Liquidity

Options trade far less frequently traded than other financial instruments. This was one of the obstacles for the investors who want to enter into options trading. Options liquidity can be measured with the help of open interest and daily volume. If options have high open interest, as more people interested in the trade, and as a result, it's more likely for us to get a better pricing for the trade.

The open interest is another tool for measuring liquidity. As option is just a contract between the buyer and the seller of option, we find new such contracts keep coming on every trading day. This gives fair idea for the investors about the number of investors showing interest in buying or selling each of the contracts. The higher the open interest of an option, the greater the indication of the liquidity of that option.

Open interest is not the only criterion to decide whether to enter into options trading of a particular security. It's the spread between the bid price and ask price that matters more for traders. The bid is the price a trader is willing to pay to purchase the option. The ask price, sometimes called the offer, is the price a trader is willing to sell the option for. The narrower the difference between those two prices, the more liquid the option is.

More Understanding about Options Time Value

Time value is basically the cost of risk paid to provide the option buyer the right to buy or sell the stock until the date the option expires. Option premiums are similar to insurance premiums; the higher the risk, the higher the premium to buy the option. As mentioned earlier, the value of option is the sum of intrinsic value and time value.

Keeping other things constant, the time value of an option is affected by both for Call & Put Options in the following ways:

* Time remaining until expiration: The longer the time to expiration, the more time value the option will have and vice versa.

* The proximity of the Strike Price to the current market price.

At-The-Money options have the greatest amount of time value as it has higher potential for intrinsic value, and the time value decreases as the intrinsic value moves to deeper In-The-Money Options and deeper Out-Of-The-Money options.

An option will not command a high time value if it is far Out-Of-The-Money as it has little chance of ending up In-The-Money. On the other hand, if an option is deep In-The-Money, it will have a smaller amount of time value as it is more likely that it will finish In-The-Money.

However, options will have a higher time value when they are At-The-Money as they have more uncertainty of finishing In-The-Money.

	Intrinsic Value	Time Value
ITM Options	As the option gets deeper ITM, Instrinsic value increases	As the option gets deeper ITM, Time value decreases
ATM Options	Zero	Time Value is at the maximum
OTM Options	Zero	As the option gets deeper OTM, Time value decreases

For both Call and Put options, the time value of an option decreases as expiration is nearing, and it decreases at an increasing rate as it is getting closer to expiration. This happens particularly for At-The-Money (ATM) options. For these options, time value decreases at a faster rate particularly during the last month before expiration.

Typically, the price movement of options will be much less than the price movement of the underlying, stock unless they are in-the-money or very close to expiration. The time value of options will be lower in cases where the stock is not expected to move greatly, such as a utility company. The opposite holds true for more volatile stocks, such as technology companies, primarily due to the uncertainty of the price of the stock before the option expires.

In general, an option loses almost a third of its value during the first half of its life and two-thirds during the second half of its life.

Chapter 2

Options Greeks

Options Greeks

Volatility

Volatility, along with timing of the expected price change, and expected direction of price, are the three variables which determine the success of an option trade. Of the three variables, volatility plays a vital role in trading options effectively. It is one of the most important principles of option trading. However, people tend to give this the least consideration when trading options. As we discussed earlier, volatility is one of the major components of option pricing.

How volatility is important in options trading

Volatility is a measure of the rate and magnitude of the change in the underlying stock's value (up or down), which is stated as a percentage over one year. A higher volatility means there is more than the average price change during a trading day, and a lower volatility means there is less than the average change in the price of stock. When it is m*athematically expressed, it is equal to the standard deviation price changes at the end of one year period.*

A stock having higher volatility would signify that the stock is more likely to have a price change, potentially moving deep in or out of the money. When volatility is high, the premium of an option will be higher. Of course, in the case of lesser volatility, a lower premium is likely to be seen. Traders would benefit by having a *good understanding of volatility. This helps them to estimate how an option is valued relating to the trends of the underlying stock.*

A stock with low volatility has a good chance of the price moving very little, if at all. Thus, volatility is an indication which tells about the likelihood of the price of a stock going up or down. Keeping other things unchanged, it is good to sell an option whose implied volatility is high and buy if its implied volatility is low.

Volatility measures market expectations regarding how the price of underlying asset is expected to trade in future. Implied volatility and historical volatility (also known as statistical volatility) are two distinct types of volatility. Using the current price of an underlying asset as a base, implied volatility reflects expected future volatility from the existing price, to the price at the expiration. Market perception of volatility for an option value in the future, is known as implied volatility. One can also project the direction of the stock price using historical volatility and fair value of the stock, along with implied volatility

Historical volatility measures the stock's volatility based on how the underlying asset had traded in the past. It refers to the past price movements of an underlying asset. Historical volatility helps in determining the possible magnitude of future moves of underlying asset. It involves a statistical calculation and tells us how quickly the price moves are in a given time frame. This is the standard deviation which analyzes the range of data points, against the average.

One can draw conclusions about the current and the future trends of option volatility by reviewing the historical volatility along with fundamental analysis. This is more important as one can calculate and expect the feasible price changes of an underlying asset in the future.

Historical volatility shows how volatility has been in the past whereas implied volatility views expected future volatility based on current option prices.

One can see the expected trading range of the market with historical volatility and implied volatility acts as an indicator of the current market sentiment.

Delta, Gamma, Theta and Vega

These are called as option greeks. They help investors to estimate risk involved in trading options. Option greeks measure price movement, interest rate movement, effect of time decay etc.

Delta

Delta provides the answer as to how the value of the option would change, with a change in stock price. Delta is a quantum of the change in the premium of an option resulting from a change in the price of the underlying asset. *Keeping other variables constant, the delta reflects how price of an option changes with a given change in the price of the underlying stock.* The value of delta ranges from one hundred to zero for puts whereas it ranges from zero to one hundred for calls. For every strike in the option chain, the sum call delta and put delta will always be one (when taken as absolute values).

Delta = % change in the option price / % change in the underlying asset price

<u>Example</u>

You have a call option at $3.50 when the stock was $55. At a stock price of $75, the option value was $4.00. The delta will be (4-3.5) / (75-74) = 0.5.

The premium on a call increases with an increase in the value of the underlying asset, keeping other things constant. *It is important for the investor to know delta values, as they help identify which options to close prior to expiration.* If an investor wants to profit from time decay, he should be sure of delta value of his position is close to zero so that the change in the price of underlying asset has little or no affect on the value of his option contract.

- Delta is not a constant as the ratio is dependent on the change in price of the underlying asset. Implied volatility can also influence the value of delta. The value of delta increases as the expiration time approaches closer.
- *L*ong puts and short stock have negative data and short puts and long stock have positive data

The following factors influence option's delta:

- Distance between stock price and the strike price; an ATM option will have a delta around 0.5, an OTM option's delta ranges between 0 and 0.5 and an OTM option's delta ranges between 0.5 and 1.
- Time to expiration; as the expiration gets shorter, the time value of the option decreases. This would result in increase of delta of ITM options
- Changes in volatility
- Changes in strike price

Gamma

G*amma explains how the delta will change relative to a move in the price of an underlying asset.* It tells us how sensitive the delta is to prices of underlying assets. Gamma helps the traders who wish to reset their positions neutral. Gamma estimates the percentage of change in delta due to the change in the price of underlying asset. The smaller the gamma, the more stable you are. It is always positive for calls and puts and negative for short calls and short puts. Stocks will not have any gamma as the delta doesn't change.

A positive gamma indicates that the delta will increase if the underlying stock also increases and have positive relationship.

A negative gamma indicates the delta will decrease when the underlying stock price increase but this has negative relationship.

Gamma will be at the highest for ATM options and it goes downwards as it moves towards ITM or OTM options. When the volatility decreases, gamma of an ATM option increases, while gamma of ITM and OTM options decreases.

Theta

Theta is a measure how fast the option loses its value expressed as the loss of time per day. It provides an estimate of how much price will be lost each day as expiration approaches, due to the lack of movement in the underlying stock price. Options that have near term expiry will have more impact and options that have longer term expiry will have lesser impact.

When the option value increases with the passage of time, is known as positive theta and when option value falls with the passage of time is known as negative theta. Theta increases as the expiration date comes closer in the case of an ATM option. As against this, theta will decrease as the expiration date comes closer. Theta of all ATM, ITM and OTM options will be zero at expiration dates.

Vega

Vega is not used as frequently by traders, however, is an important dimension.

Vega represents how much the correlation in the change in the value of an option with a change in volatility of the underlying stock. Risk exposure is expressed numerically to changes as implied volatility. Any decrease in the implied volatility would benefit the traders. An increase in implied volatility will result in an increase in the price of an underlying asset while a decrease in implied volatility decreases an option's price.

As higher volatility results in higher option price, any positive change in the implied volatility will create profit for the option buyers.

A positive vega: Volatility increase results in an increase in the price of underlying asset. The vega of long call and put will be positive. Vega will be higher for options that have longer life. An ATM option will have greater vega, while ITM and OTM options have a lower vega.

A negative Vega: option price decreases with an increase in the volatility and increases with decrease in volatility.

Vega is highest for ATM options and decreases for ITM and OTM options. Any change in volatility will change the ATM options most.

Chapter 3

Stocks vs. Options

Stocks vs. Options

Stock gives right of ownership in the company whereas an option is a contract giving right to buy or sell a stock at a specified price in a given period of time. A share of stock is a unit of ownership, which is created by the company and is traded on and exchange such as the New York Stock Exchange. Options are neither issued by the company nor by any exchange. Options are created by investors (the buyer and seller) and expire after a predetermined time frame.

Trading in stocks can be compared with gambling where the investor will be betting on the share price of that particular stock. If the price goes up, all shareholders will benefit and vice versa. But there will be losers and gainers in options trading.

Trading in stocks is straight forward and much easier than trading in options. Option trading is much more complex, inherently more risky, and requires additional knowledge, as they are more volatile in nature. An investor typically needs to submit additional documents to a brokerage firm in order to trade in options.

Stock trading is simple and has single dimension whereas option trading is multi-dimensional (it depends on stock price, time decay and the volatility).

The value of an option becomes worthless on its expiration date. However, you find no such expiration date with a stock. You can hold a stock position indefinitely, and can close it any time by selling it at the current market price.

The monetary loss from option trading will be much less than those arising from trading the stock, assuming that the same number of equivalent share are traded, as you invest only the margin money. You can also realize greater returns compared to trading in stocks.

Options trading can be a good alternative for those people who are not comfortable with trading stocks due to significant capital requirement.

To profit from stock options, direction of price movement of the underlying stock is important. In addition, in options trading, you need to anticipate the magnitude of the price movement. Options will give you higher leverage compared to stocks. For example, you own one-hundred shares of ABC bought at $100 per share last month. If its price is $120 today, the net profit is twenty percent, in one month. Let us assume that one month ago you bought a $100 call option (At the Money) for $8, which as we learned earlier is almost all time value. If the stock performed exactly the same, the intrinsic value of the option would have increased by the $20 appreciation of the stock price. However, the option premium would have lost one month of time value. Depending on how long the option has until expiration, this could be some, or all, of the original $8 premium. The net result would be percentage gains that far exceed what you would have earned with the stock.

As options can create great profits, they also can create significant losses. Instead of stock going to $120, if it goes to $80, the call option would have become worthless and you lose entire $8 per share, resulting in a loss of one-hundred percent of your initial investment. If you purchased the stock, you would have only lost twenty percent.

It is possible to use options in a certain way that the inherent benefits of stocks trading can be achieved by using some smart options strategies. This is explained later in the book, in the chapter titled "Best Strategies".

Chapter 4

Key to Success

Why Selling is the key to success

If there is one way that the most people lose money, it lies in buying options, whether they are call or put options. This is confirmed by a study performed by the CME.

"Option traders rarely take into account a little known underlying fact about these derivative markets as most of the options expire at Out-Of-The-Money. A study analyzing three years of data compiled by the Chicago Mercantile Exchange (CME) confirms it.

That means buyers lose on most option trades. Given this option market reality, serious option traders should consider developing a net option selling (writing) approach to take advantage of this tendency.

Three key patterns emerge from the study of CME data;

1. On average, three out of every four options held to expiration end up worthless.
2. The share of puts and calls that expired worthless is influenced by the primary trend of the underlying market.
3. Option sellers still come out ahead even when the seller is going against the trend.

Based on a CME study of expiring and exercised options covering a period of three years (1997, 1998, 1999), an average of 76.5 percent of all options held to expiration in five markets expired worthless (Out-Of-The-Money). The number remained consistent for the three year period.

The actual numbers for five markets show more than twenty million expired (worthless) options and a little more than six million exercised (in-the-money) options. Options that are In-The-Money at expiration are exercised automatically. Therefore, we can derive total expired worthless options by subtracting those exercised from total options held to expiration. A closer look at the data reveals certain patterns, such as how a trend bias in the underlying affects the share of call options vs. put options expiring worthless. Clearly, however, the overall pattern in that most options expired worthless.

As a whole, S&P 500 put options recorded the highest percentage with 82.6% expiring out of the money or worthless. This percentage was above the average for the entire study—76.5% of all CME futures options expired worthless—and is due to the stock index options on futures (NASDAQ 100 and S&P 500) having very large number of put options expiring worthless—more than 90 percent.

This bias in favor of put sellers can be attributed to the strong bullish bias of the stock indexes during the period although there were some sharp but short-lived market declines. Data for 2001–2003, however, would no doubt show a shift toward more calls expiring worthless, reflecting the change in a primary bear, market trend since 2000. "[1]

Here are some of the main reasons in favor of options selling vs. buying:

1. Going against the trend

As is obvious from the above article that even if you end up going against the trend, the odds are in your favor for Out-Of-The-Money options expiring worthless, while it is absolutely opposite for the option buyers.

---

[1] Summa, John F., "Option Sellers vs. Buyers; Who wins?"
Futures Magazine Mar. 2003: 52–55

2. Not controlled by greed

When you buy options, you may be controlled by the greed as it may be difficult to determine when the trend may reverse itself. You may end up selling the option either too early or too late. This may not be the case when you sell put options as in the worst case scenario you may end up owning the stock at a lower price than you may have intended to buy it at in the first place.

3. No Stop Losses

When you buy options, you may put stop losses below or above a certain price. You may have done it based on a technical or fundamental analysis. How many times did it happen that the market will go down or go up to your stop loss point, take you out of the market and then reversed the direction?

You may not have to place a stop loss order when you sell puts as in the worst case you will end up owning the stock at a price that you intended to buy at.

4. Time in your favor

This is one of biggest advantage of selling options instead of buying it. It has been discussed in previous chapters that every option has two values. One is intrinsic value and the other being the time value. Even if the stock does not move against the trend, time value of the options will keep on eroding every day. The option having less value on a daily basis hurts the buyer of the option, while the opposite is true when you sell options. The seller is a gainer every day, even if the stock does not move at all.

5. Earn interest on other's money

When you sell options, it adds up money in your account. Even though you may not be able to withdraw it, you earn interest on the money every day until the day of expiration. The opposite is true when you buy options. In this regard, you have to be very careful in selecting the right brokerage company. Many brokerage companies do not pay interest on the money which is accumulated by selling options.

Down side of selling Options

1. Unlimited Risk

When you buy options, your maximum loss is limited to the amount of the money that you paid to buy those options. The opposite can be true for the seller of the options. The seller is exposed to potentially having to buy back the option at a much higher price. However, there are ways to control this unlimited part of the risk by using several strategies which will be discussed in the chapters to follow.

2. Limited Profit

With respect to potential profit, the seller of an option definitely has a disadvantage. The seller cannot possibly make more than the amount that he sold the option for.

Chapter 5

Bullish Strategies

These strategies have been presented for academic reasons. This shall not constitute a recommendation of these strategies to any individual.

Long Call

Call buying (Long Call) is considered to be a speculative strategy by most investors. In a long strategy, an investor will pay a premium to purchase a contract giving them the right to buy stock at a set strike price .The investor needs the underlying security to move higher in order to gain a profit.

Advantages with Long Options

Potential Profits can be infinite.

Long Option positions are highly leveraged. Investors can control shares of a security for about ten percent of the securities value.

The maximum risk is the cost of the option.

Disadvantages with Long Options

Long Options positions offer no downside protection, as one might have with a Covered Call trade, even though the maximum risk is low.

Long Options are a depreciating asset. The value will always decrease as the expiration date approaches.

Timing when entering a Long Option trade is critical as time is always working against the investor in this strategy.

Call Buying (Long Calls)

This is a bullish to extremely bullish strategy. In a Long Call position, the investor expects the stock to rise. As the underlying security increases, the value of the Call will increase as well. Purchasing a Call gives the investor the right to buy shares of stock at a set price (strike price). A Call option investor is looking to take advantage of the stock movement without investing a large amount of capital to own the stock.

A more conservative investor may buy an ITM (strike below the stock price) or ATM Call; speculative investors may buy OTM (strike above the stock price) hoping for a large return.

Profits are theoretically unlimited as the stock could go up infinitely.

Example

The closing price of Intermune Inc. (ITMN) common stock was $10.47 November 21, 2008. Based on that price, you may choose to buy an April 10 strike call option at a cost of $5.60. Of course that price is per share which means $560 for the option contract (one contract equals one-hundred shares).

The total cost is $560.

The maximum risk is $560.

The maximum profit is unlimited.

The break even point is calculated by adding the strike price to the initial premium paid (break even point = $10.47 + $5.60 = $16.07).

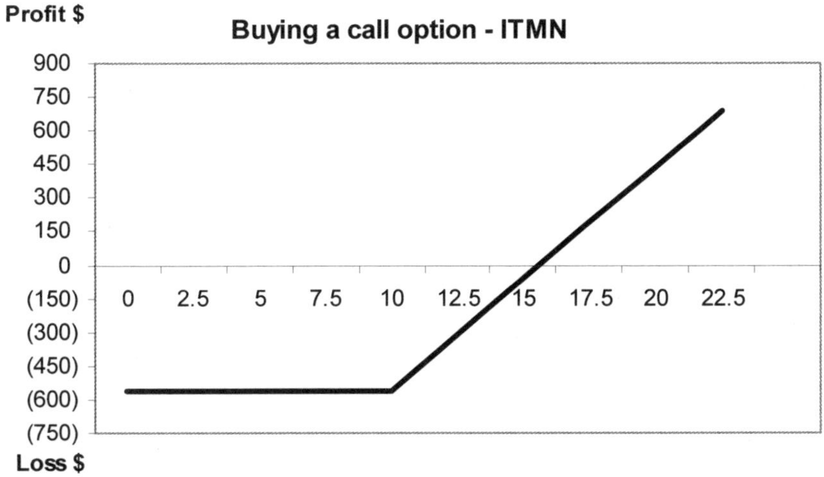

You would the following formula to determine the net result of an option if held to expiration:

[(M - S) - P] / P = net result per share.

M = Current Market Price per share at expiration,

S = Strike Price of option,

P = option premium.

Using the above formula, if ITMN stock closes at $10 at expiration date, returns are: [(10-10)] – 5.60] / 5.60 = $0.00 per share, which is a loss of one hundred percent.

If the stock closes at $20 at expiration date, returns are: [(20-10)] – 5.60] / 5.60 = $4.40 per share, which is a gain of seventy nine percent.

Example

If ABCs stock price expected to go up from the current $9.50 to $11.00 or more over the next two months, you may decide to buy an ATM call option. You can buy a Jan $9.00 call @ $0.25.

Your profit if the stock price reaches $11.00 would be calculated as follows: [(11.00-9.50) – 0.25] = $1.25 per share. This is equal to 500 percent of your investment.

Your Breakeven Point is calculated as follows: 9.50 + 0.25 = 9.75.

Your Maximum risk = $0.25 per share

Synthetic Long Stock

A synthetic long stock is a bullish strategy with combination of long call and a short put of the same series. It is established by shorting an At-The-Money Put and buying an At-The-Money Call. If the cost of buying the call is greater than the money taken in from selling the put, it is also called a debit spread. If the call costs less than the premium received from selling the put, it is then called a credit spread. This option position is said to be comparable to a long stock where the strike price of both long call and short put options is the same. If the underlying stock drops, the call expires Out-Of-The-Money and when the value of the short increases, it loses its extrinsic value.

Synthetic Long Stock = Long Call + Short Put

You will be exposed to unlimited profits as well as potentially significant losses when you buy a stock. However, you lose nothing if the price remains stagnant. The premium received form short put covers the premium paid on the long call. The call option gives exposure to unlimited profits where as short put option is exposed to a potentially significant loss.

Margin requirements on the short put and long call combination will vary, and depends on the volatility of the price of the underlying stock. Generally it will not be more than 10 percent of the value of the exercise price of the options. Therefore, you can leverage 90 percent of the stock.

Here is how one would calculate the Break Even Point. If calculating for a debit spread; Call strike price + spread debit = Break Even. If calculating for a credit spread; Put strike price - spread credit = Break Even.

Maximum Risk = the strike price of the put, plus the cost of the call, less the premium received from selling the put, multiplied by the number of contracts.

Example

An ABC share is currently trading at $19.44, while Jan 19 calls are $0.94 and Jan 19 puts are $0.52.,

Long Stock: Profit if the share price move to $24 for 100 shares = (2,400 -$1,944) = $456

Synthetic Long Stock: Profit if a call option is bought and put option is sold would $5.00 (difference between strike price and market price at expiration) - $0.94 (the cost of the call) + $0.52 (premium received for selling put) = $4.58 per share, or $458 for the contract of one hundred shares.

As you can see, the profit is almost identical to owning the stock, but required a significantly smaller commitment of money.

Now, let's see what would happen if the stock was $15 on expiration:

-$4.44 (difference between strike price and market price at expiration) + $0.52 (premium received from selling put) - $0.94 (cost of call) = loss of $4.86 per share, or $486 for the contract of 100 shares.

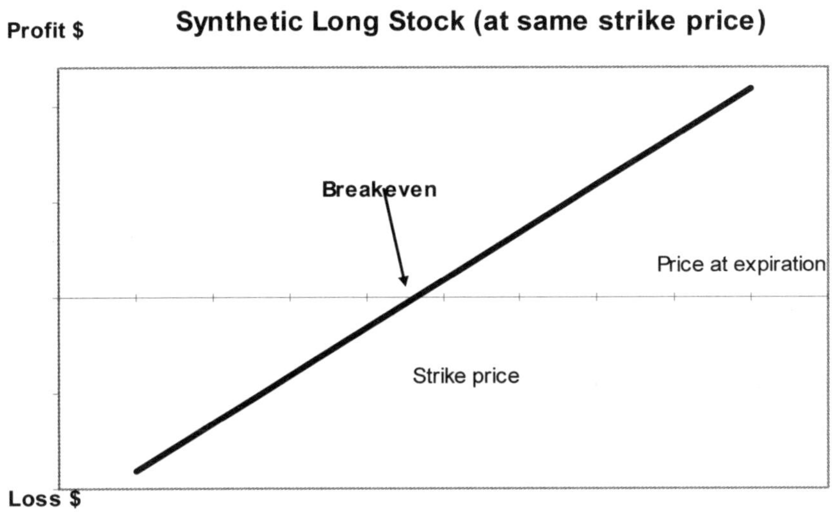

The drawback of this strategy is that when the stock pays dividend, you do not receive it. There is a possibility of early assignment if the price fall so much that the naked put becomes deep-in-the-money.

Synthetic Long Stock = Long Call + Naked Put Sell

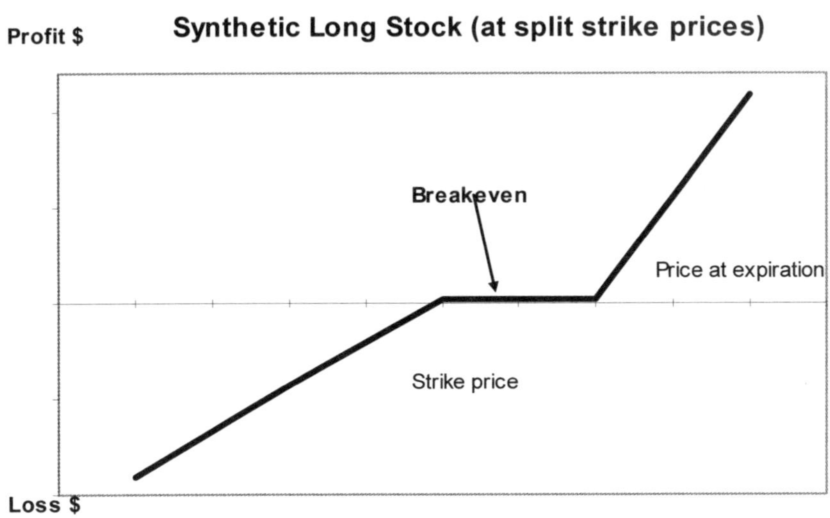

A new synthetic position would need to be established in order to continue participating in the stock price movement, once the options expire.

Deep-In-The-Money Put

A put option is said to be deep In-The-Money when the strike price is much higher than the price of the underlying asset. The delta of this put will be close to one and any change in the value of the underlying asset, a similar amount of change takes place in the option until stock price nears the strike price of the put.

The possibility of early assignment can be a major drawback to this stock substitute. The position can be established again if the position is assigned early. It is better not to pick a strike price that is too deep In-The-Money so that put price would include some time value. If there is not much open interest, the possibility of early assignment can be reduced.

Example

ABC stock is trading at $13.25 in October. A January 15 put is selected in order to participate in the upward movement of the stock and sold for $3.15 per share.

This results a credit of $315. The time value of the option premium is (13.25 + 3.15) – 15.00 = $1.40 per share.

The margin requirement is 25 percent of the stock price (as the naked put is ITM) + price of Jan put. It is $646.25 [(13.25x25%) + 3.25] multiplied by 100. This is much less than the required money if you were to buy the stock.

If the stock were to remain at $13.25 until expiration, the option would be exercised at the $15 strike. You, being short the option, would be forced to purchase the stock at $15. Assuming it were to be immediately sold, the result would be a loss of $1.75 per share, or $1,750. However, this amount would be offset by the premium received of $3.15 per share, for a net gain of $1.40 per share or $1,400. In this case, since the stock price at expiration is the same as the price it was when the option was opened, the profit is the time value.

In order to profit on this, or any, short put, the price of the stock must remain higher than the strike price of the option, less the premium. It is also important to remember that there is significant risk for loss with short puts. If the stock in the above example were to go to $0, then the investor who shorted the put would be forced to buy worthless stock at $15, having only received the premium for his troubles. This would result in a loss of $11.85 per share, or $1,185.

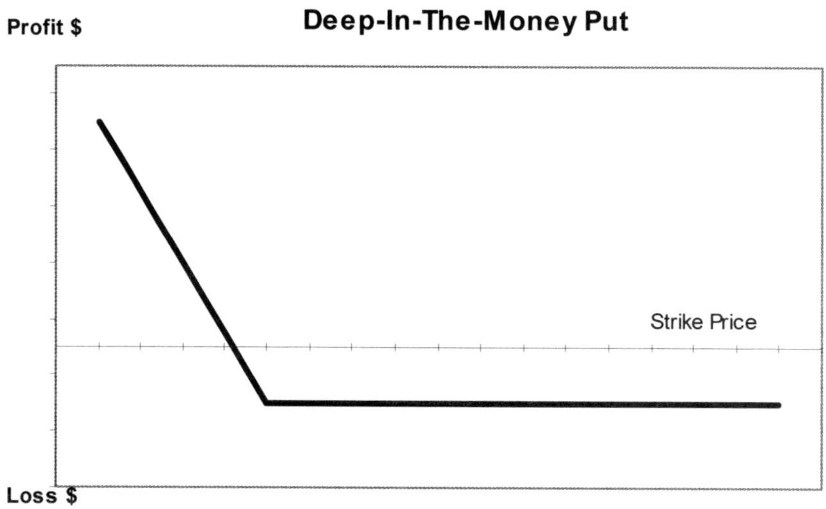

Collars

The Collar Spread is similar to the Covered Call trade, except an investor will purchase a Put to protect against a sudden decline on the stock. Like the Covered Call, the Collar Spread is a neutral to bullish strategy. But, there are many different combinations of the Call and Put option that an investor can use to help them limit the risk and maximize their returns.

In a Standard Collar Spread, an investor will buy shares of stock and then sell an ATM or OTM Call against those shares, just like a Covered Call trade. Then, the investor will purchase an OTM Put for the same expiration month as the Call that was sold. The primary risk in a covered Call strategy is that the underlying stock may decline faster than we can collect premium. By purchasing an OTM Put option we can protect the position from a large drastic decline in the stock price. The covered Call sale helps finance the purchase of the Put option. This strategy offers greater protection and is considered more conservative than a similar Covered Call trade, but some of the return is sacrificed when the investor purchases the Put option for extra protection.

Since the loss in the stock price is limited by the Put, a maximum loss can be calculated. Below is an example of a Standard Collar.

The closing price of Citigroup (ticker symbol: C) shares was $3.77 on Nov 21st 2008. To create a collar, following positions would be taken.

Sell 1 contract of (C Mar 2009 5 Call) @ $1.50 ($150.00).

Buy 100 shares of C (Citigroup Inc.) @ $3.77 $377.00.

Buy 1 contract of (C Mar 2009 2.5 Put) @ $1.09 $109.00.

The total Cost is $336.

The maximum risk is $86.

Net Premium is calculated as follows: call bid price - put ask price ($1.50 - $1.09 = $0.41).

Net Debit is calculated as follows: Stock Price - Net Premium ($3.77 - $0.41 = $3.36.

Maximum Risk is calculated as follows: Stock Price - Put Strike - Net Credit ($3.77 - $2.50 - $041 = $0.86 per share, or $86.00).

% Maximum Risk = Maximum Risk / Net Debit = $0.86 / $3.36 = 7.2%.

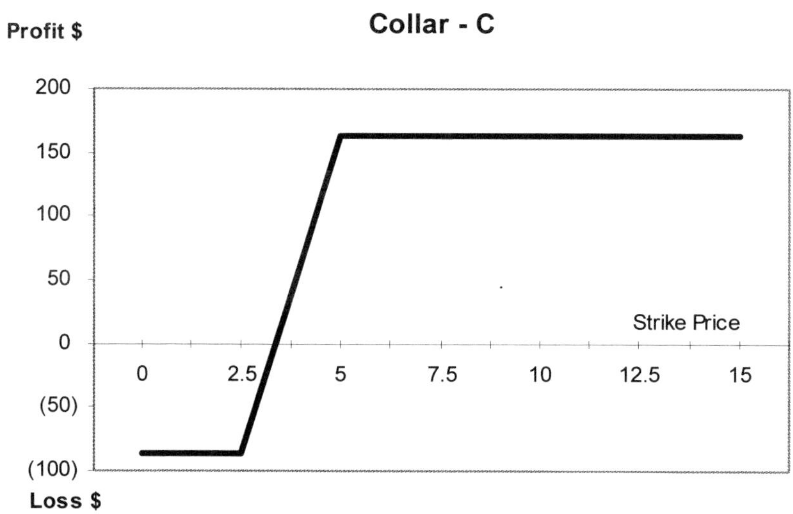

Break Even = Net Debit (for a Standard Collar) = $3.36.

% Break Even = Stock Price - Net Debit / Stock Price = $3.77 - $3.36 / $3.77 = 10.87%.

Maximum Profit = Net Premium + Stock Profit/Loss = $0.41 + ($5.00 - $3.77) = $1.64.

Although this is what is defined as a Standard Collar trade, there are many different combinations that can be used to build a Collar strategy. The investor could decide to buy an In-the-Money Put for extra protection and sell a deep Out-of-the-Money Call in the same month to counter some of the cost of the Put. This is referred to as a "Debit Collar" or "Standard Debit Collar" as both options has the same expiration month. Below is an example of a Debit Collar.

Taking the Citigroup example,

Sell 1 contract of (C Mar 2009 7.5 Call) @ $0.94 ($94.00).

Buy 100 shares of C (Citigroup Inc.) @ $3.77 $377.00.

Buy 1 contract of (C Mar 2009 5 Put) @ $2.80 = $280.00.

Net Premium = Call Bid price - Put Ask price = $0.94 - $2.80= $-1.86 (debit).

Net Debit = Stock Price - Net Premium = $3.77 - (-$1.86) = $5.63.

Maximum Risk = Stock Price - Put Strike - Net Credit = $3.77 - $5.00 - (-$1.86) = $0.63 per share, or $63.00.

% Maximum Risk = Maximum Risk / Net Debit = $0.63 / $5.63= 11.2%.

Break Even = Net Debit (for a Standard Debit Collar) = $5.63.

% Break Even = Stock Price - Net Debit / Stock Price = $3.77 - $5.63 / $3.77 = -49%.

(A negative % to Break Even means the breakeven price is above the current stock price).

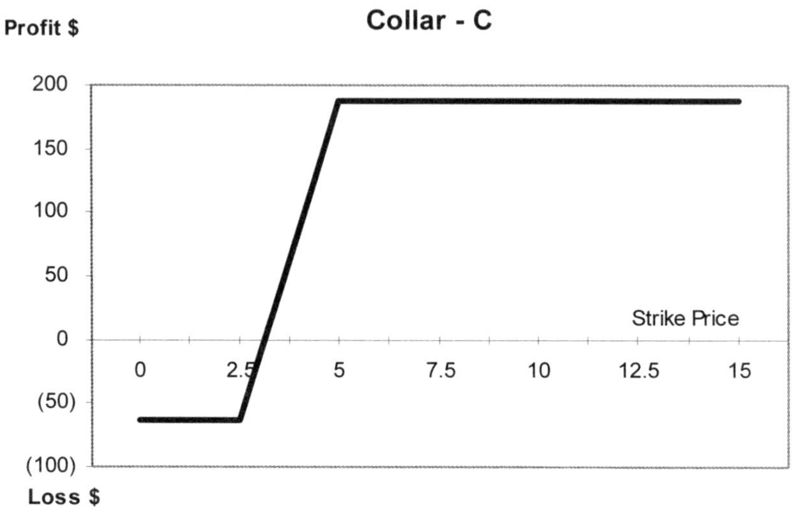

Maximum Profit = Net Premium + Stock Profit/Loss = $-1.86+ ($7.50 - $3.77) = $1.87.

% gain if Assigned = (Max Profit) / (Net Debit) = $1.87/ $5.63 = 33.2%.

In the Debit Collar spread the investor is risking a much lower amount while having a higher percentage return, if assigned. The Debit Collar offers much greater protection and lower monetary risk, but there is also a lower probability of earning the higher return. Each investor will have their own personal Risk/Reward tolerance as to what they wish to risk, what type of return they want to achieve, and then compare that against the probability of making that return.

In addition to adjusting the Call and the Put strike price for a Collar trade on a given stock, some investors like to purchase the Put option with an expiration further out in time than that of the short Call. This is due to one of the fundamental rules of option investing: Investors will increase their annualized return when they sell month by month, and will decrease their annualized cost if they buy an option further out in time. If an investor was planning on holding the stock for a three, six or twelve month period, they might be able to lower the cost of protection by purchasing a Put that is three, six, or twelve months out in time.

Example

Sell 1 contract of (C Jan 2009 10 Call) @ $0.50 = ($50.00).

Buy 1 contract of (C Jun 2009 7.5 Put) @ $1.87 = $187.00.

Buy 100 shares of C on Dec 8th 2008 @ $8.18 = $818.00.

Net Premium = Call Bid price - Put Ask price = $1.87 - $0.50 = $-1.37 (debit).

Net Debit = Stock Price - Net Premium = $8.18 - (-$1.37) = $9.55.

Maximum Risk = Stock Price - Put Strike - Net Credit = $8.18 - $7.50 - (-$1.37) = $2.05.

% Maximum Risk = Maximum Risk / Net Debit = $2.05 / $10.00 = 20.5%.

Break Even = Stock Price where theoretical value of Long Put + remaining position value equals the Net Debit. For this example, the Break Even = $7.82.

(For Collars where the Put is farther out in time, the Black-Scholes pricing model is used to calculate the Break Even price, as the Put option will have remaining time value).

% Break Even = Stock Price - Theoretical Break Even/ Stock Price = $8.18 - $7.82 / $8.18 = 4.5%

Trade Details	Cost Basis	Expected Value	Expected Profit/Loss
· Sell 1 CAB (C Jan 2009 10 Call)	($50.00)	$0.00	$50.00
· Buy 1 CRQ (C Jun 2009 7.5 Put)	$187.00	$160.00	($27.00)
· Buy 100 C (Citigroup Inc.)	$818.00	$818.00	$0.00
Total Expected Profit/Loss			$23.00

Maximum Profit = Net Premium + Stock Profit/Loss = -$1.37 + $0.37 = $1.54.

(This maximum profit does not take into account any theoretical remaining value of the long Put).

(The Black-Scholes pricing model is used to calculate the remaining Put value).

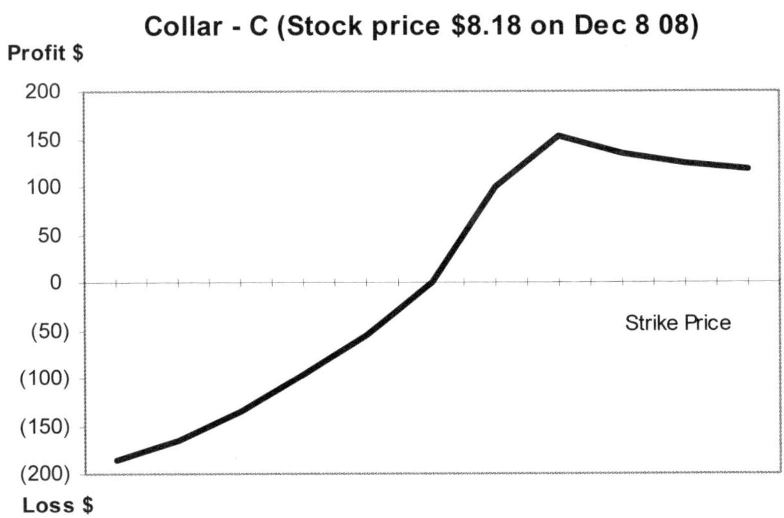

Just like the other Collar examples, the maximum profit is achieved when the stock is trading right at the short Call strike price at the near term expiration date. Remember, an investor who enters a Collar position where the Put is further out in time is looking to save on premium on an annualized basis, most likely they are planning on holding the stock for an extended period of time or they have a specific methodology designed to roll the Call position month by month. There are various other combinations that be used, both to be more conservative and to be more aggressive.

Married Puts

Introduction

The Married Put strategy is also referred to as a Protective Put. In a Married Put strategy an investor will purchase shares of the underlying stock while purchasing put contracts that correspond (remember one contract equals one hundred shares) to the number of shares purchased. This is done to "protect" the long shares of the underlying security. The purchased put acts as insurance for the underlying shares as they have purchased the right to sell the shares of stock at the strike price between the time of purchase and the expiration date of the put.

The investor is purchasing the stock and the corresponding number of puts, creating an overall net debit for the position. The total out of pocket value to enter into a Married Put trade is equal to the price of the stock plus the premium of the put option. This value is referred to as the Net Debit. The maximum profit for the position is unlimited as the stock could rise infinitely. The maximum monetary value at risk is equal to the net debit for the position minus the strike price of the purchased put.

Investors use the Married Put strategy to protect shares of stock against large drops in the underlying stock. This is a bullish strategy, as the investor is looking for an increase in the underlying stock price to earn a profit. The purchased put gives the investor extra insurance on the position for an additional cost. In order to implement the strategy, one would:

Buy shares of an underlying security.

Buy the corresponding number of put contracts against the purchased shares.

The sum of the stock price and the put premium is the net debit.

The maximum risk is equal to the net debit minus the put strike price.

The maximum profit is unlimited as the stock could rise infinitely.

The Break Even point is equal to the net debit.

Profit is realized when the stock rises above the Break Even point.

Calculation for the Married Put Strategy is:

% Max Risk = Maximum Risk / Net Debit

Example – 1

Fairchild Semiconductor International, Inc. (FCS) had a closing price on November 21, 2008 of $3.20.

Buy 100 shares of FCS @ $3.20 = $320.00.

Buy 1 contract of (FCS May 2009 5 Put) @ $2.10 = $210.00.

Net Debit = Stock Price + Put Ask Price.

Net Debit = $3.20 + $2.10 = $5.30.

Break Even = Net Debit.

Break Even = $5.30.

Maximum Risk = Net Debit - Put Strike Price.

Maximum Risk = $5.30 - $5.00 = $0.30.

% Max Risk = $0.30 / $5.30 = 0.06%.

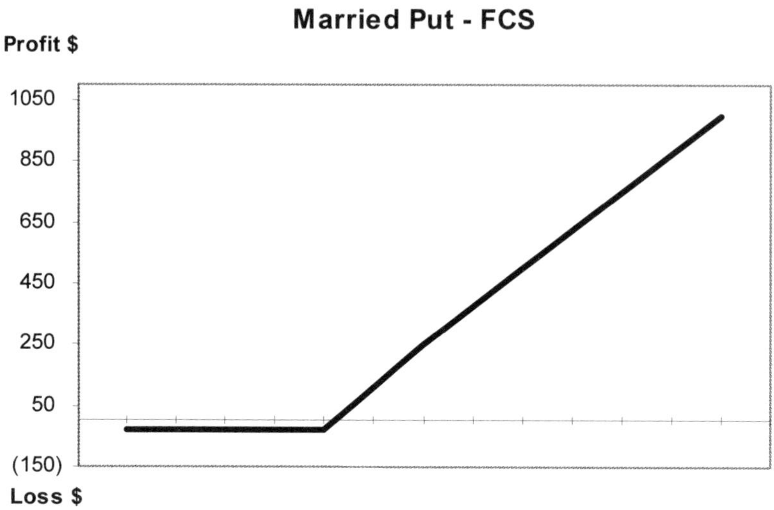

This example is an In-the-Money Married Put example. The strike price of the put is higher than the current underlying stock price. This would give the investor the right, but not the obligation, to sell their shares of stock at $5.00 at any time between now and the expiration date, regardless of the then current market price. However, because the put is ITM, the investor has to pay a higher premium because of the intrinsic value.

Example – 2

Buy 100 shares of FCS@ $3.20 = $320.00.

Buy 1 contract of (FCS May 2009 2.5 Put) @ $0.40 = $40.00.

Total Cost = $360.
Net Debit = $3.20 + $0.40 = $3.60.
Break Even = $3.60.
Maximum Risk = $3.60 - $2.50 = $1.10.

% Max Risk = $1.10 / $3.60 = 30.5%.

Maximum Profit = Unlimited

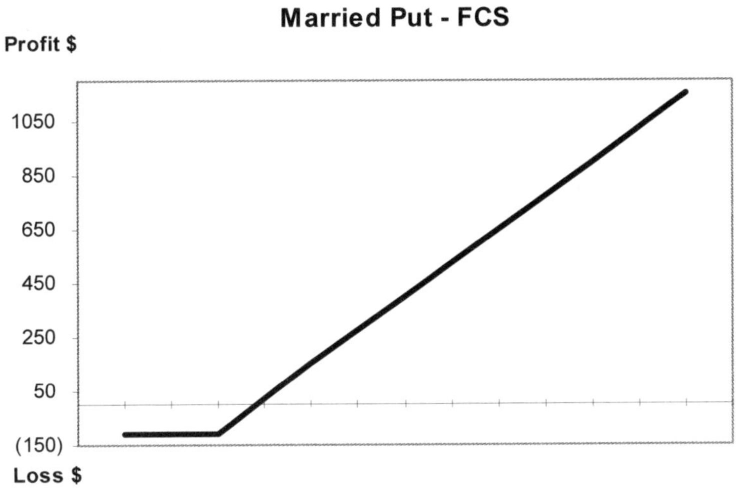

The OTM Married Put in example 2 has a lower ask price, thus the position has a lower Break Even value, but a much higher maximum risk. Because the 2.5 put is OTM, the stock is not protected until it drops below $2.50 per share.

In both of these examples, the puts available are either considerably in the money, or considerably out of the money. Some investors choose to utilize this strategy when the put is at the money, or very close to at the money. This means that virtually the entire option premium is time value.

Example

Buy 100 shares of MSFT on January 2, 2008 @ $20.33 per share = $2,033.

Buy 1 February 20 Put @ $1.37 = $137.

Net Debit (Total Cost) = $2,170.
Net Debit = $20.33 + $1.37 = $21.70.

Break Even = \$21.70.

Maximum Risk = \$20.33 - \$20.00 = \$0.33 per share.

% Max Risk = \$0.33 / \$20.33 = 1.6%.

Maximum Profit = Unlimited.

Advantages of this Strategy

The potential profits are unlimited.

The maximum loss is limited due to the protection of the put.

Married Puts allows investors to enter a long stock position with low percentage risk.

This strategy provides safety against a surprise gap down due to an unexpected news announcement.

Disadvantages of this Strategy

The investor will have to pay an additional premium for the extra protection.

Although the strategy greatly reduces risk, it does not erase all risk.

Bull Call Debit Spread

Introduction

This is one of the bullish strategies, where an investor will sell an At the Money (ATM) or slightly In the Money (ITM) CALL then buy a deeper ITM CALL. Since the CALL that is purchased is deeper ITM, the transaction results in a net debit.

BUY a deep ITM (In the Money) CALL.

Sell a Call, in the same expiration month, that is ATM, or slightly ITM but with a higher strike price than the long call.

The net investment is the net debit (difference in premiums).

The maximum risk is the net debit (difference in premiums).

The maximum profit is realized if the stock is anywhere above the higher strike price. Maximum profit is equal to the difference in the strike prices minus the net debit.

The break even point is the lower strike price (#1) plus the net debit. A profit is realized at any price above the break even point.

Maximum profit is made when the stock price rises above the highest strike price (#2 CALL).

Profit is achieved when both legs of the position are liquidated prior to expiration.

The return calculations for the Bull Call Debit Spread are:

% Return = Maximum profit ÷ Net Investment.

% Return = (Difference in strike prices - Net Debit) ÷ Net Debit.

Net Debit = Premium on Bought Call - Premium on Sold Call.

Example

Wal-Mart Stores Inc. (WMT) had a share price $51.46 on November 21, 2008.

Buy 1 contract of (WMT Jun 2009 45 Call) @ $12.95 = $1,295.00.

Sell 1 contract of (WMT Jun 2009 50 Call) @ $9.65 = $965.00.

Net Debit (Total Cost) = $330.

% Return = (Difference in strikes - Net Debit) ÷ Net Debit.

% Return = (50 - 45 - 3.30) ÷ 3.30 = 1.70 ÷ 3.30 = 51.5%.

Max. Risk = Net Debit = $12.95 - $9.65 = $3.30, if stock is lower than $45.

% Maximum Risk = 100%.

Max. Profit = Difference in strikes - Net Debit = 5.00 - 3.30 = 1.70, if stock is greater than $50.

Break Even = Lower Strike + Net Debit = $45.00 + $3.30 = $48.30.

Maximum Profit = $170.

Advantages of this strategy

This is a BULLISH strategy, as the profit can only be realized when the stock price is above the break even point.

If the stock goes very high gains are limited to the difference in strikes minus the debit.

Losses are limited to the net debit.

No stock is actually owned. (Uncovered position)

In the money (ITM) calls offer lower break even points, but limit profits.

Out of the money calls offer larger profits, but have higher break even points, which require a greater rise in the price of the stock to realize gains.

Calendar Call Spread

Introduction

Calendar Calls are a bullish strategy. A conservative investor will look to trade Calendar LEAP spreads by purchasing an In the Money (ITM) one-year or two-year LEAP and then selling an At the Money (ATM) or an Out of the Money (OTM) near term calls against the LEAP (diagonal spread). Basically, this strategy is a leveraged covered call position because the investor will pay less for the LEAP than they would to own the stock. A profit is realized if the stock is trading above the Break Even point at expiration. Since the ITM LEAP will always cost more than the short call, the position is entered at a debit. An investor can also trade horizontal spreads where the strikes of the two options are the same, but have different expiration dates.

The break even point is the point at which the value of the bought call will equal the net debit. A profit is realized at any price above the break even point.

The return calculations for the Calendar Call Spread are:

% if Assigned = Maximum Profit ÷ Net Investment.

% if Assigned = (Long Call Value - Net Debit) ÷ Net Debit.

% of Downside Protection = Premium Income ÷ Buy Price of Long Contracts.

% if Unchanged. = [Long Call Value (at short-term exp. w/ current stock price) - Net Debit] ÷ Net Debit.

% of Downside Protection = Short Call Bid ÷ Long Call Ask.

Example

You buy a long call at a specified price, preferably at a lower strike price and sell a near month call at equal to the strike price of long call or more strikes than long call.

Entergy Corp. (ETR) had a stock price of $81.28 on December 8, 2008.

Buy 1 contract of (ETR Jun 2009 80 Call) @ $14.40 = $1,440.00.

Sell 1 contract of (ETR Jan 2009 90 Call) @ $2.65 = ($265.00).

The net debit, or total cost, is the net amount debited to your account. This is equal to the difference of premiums.

Net Debit (Total Cost) = $1,175.

The maximum risk is the net debit which is equal to the difference of premiums.

Maximum Risk = Net Debit = 14.60 – 2.70 = $11.75 per share.

The maximum profit can be realized when the stock price trades at the near month call strike price. This will be equal to the difference of the long option at near term expiration and the net debit.

Maximum Profit = Long Call Value - Net Debit = 540.

Long Call Value = Utilize the Black-Scholes model for determining the value of the long call when the stock price is at the higher strike.

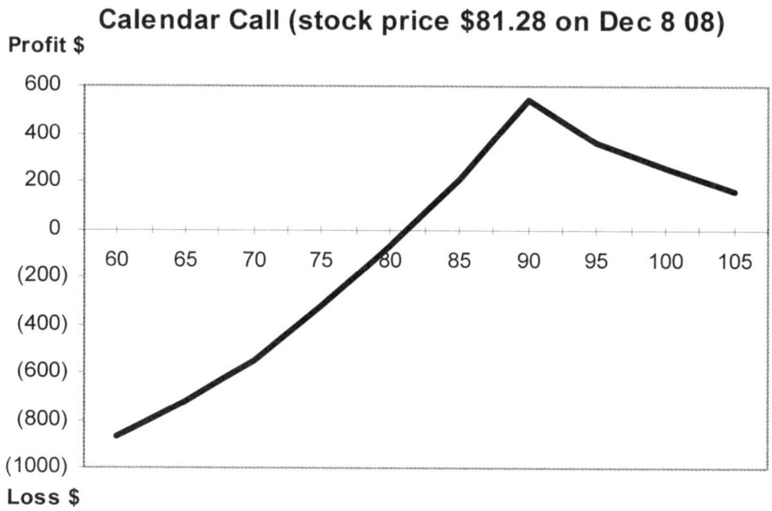

Determining the long option value for percentage return if assigned and percentage if unchanged:

When the short-term option is in-the-money and nearing expiration, it is usually more profitable to buy stock on the open market to cover the obligation rather than exercising the long-term option. This is because the long-term option will most likely have some time value left. As a result, it can be more profitable to sell the long-term option rather than exercise it. Doing so enables you to recapture time value.

Advantages / Disadvantages of this strategy

This is a BULLISH strategy, the profit can only be realized when the stock price is above the break even point.

Buying the LEAP in lieu of the stock can generally allow the stock to be controlled at a discount. In this case the LEAP is purchased for 40 percent of the stock price, with very little time premium. For options that are nearer term than LEAPs, this advantage will apply less.

Losses are limited to the net debit.

No stock is actually owned (Uncovered Position).

One of the principal advantages of this strategy is that one can potentially write the near term calls many times before the expiration of the bought call that expires further out in time. Therefore, the investors' cost for the long call can be greatly reduced by the accumulated premiums received from selling multiple shorter term calls.

Cautions with this strategy

If the stock goes very high gains are limited to the difference in strikes minus the debit.

If the stock goes very high immediately there is the possibility of actually losing money if the near term call is assigned. Therefore, it is important that the difference in strike prices be greater than the initial net debit to assure a profit if the spread is assigned early during the first write.

Practically speaking, it may be difficult to write a near term call for every write cycle.

Long Put to Protect Your Stock (Protective Put)

Introduction

When you own stock and buy a put of the underlying stock to defend against fall in the price of underlying stock, it is know as a protective put. The seller receives the premium and is obligated to receive the stock if you want to exercise the option by the expiration date. This implies that the position must outperform the amount of money that is paid as premium. Purchasing puts and holding shares of underlying stock simultaneously is a directional bullish strategy. Since the investor believes the stock should trade higher, the protective put is generally an ATM or OTM put in order to reduce its cost.

You, own the stock, as a protective put investor. Your risk is limited even if the price falls as you know your minimum selling price. You have unlimited profit potential, once the stock price goes above the cost of position. However, you cannot profit until stock price go above the cost of stock plus the cost of acquiring put. Moreover, you should always remember that put does have a finite life.

The protective put investor retains all benefits ownership until it is sold. The protective put limits the potential downside loss by guaranteeing a minimum sale price prior to expiration.

Protective Put Strategy

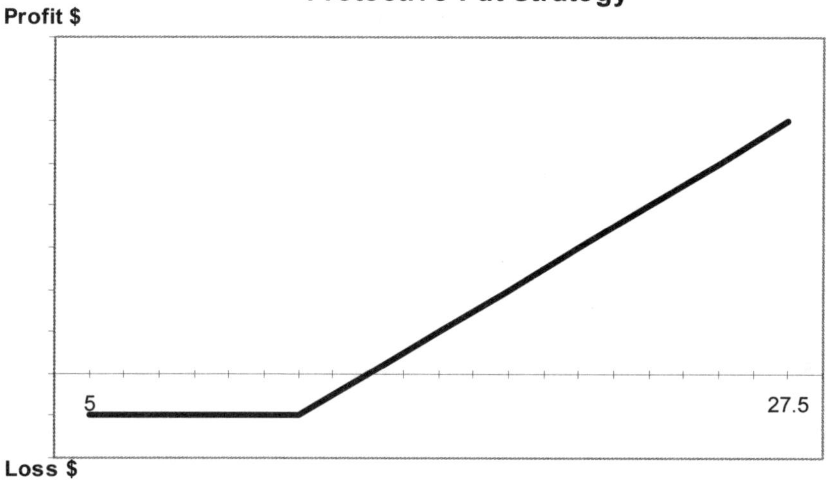

Buying a protective put option is appropriate when you believe that the underlying stock that you own may take a significant fall, but you do not wish to sell your shares. It would also be appropriate if you were uncomfortable carrying the risk of the entire long position, particularly if it is a larger than normal position. Normally, you would buy enough options to cover the number of shares of the underlying stock that you own.

Example

Let's look at Dow Chemical (DOW) stock trading at $15.41. It would take $1,541 to buy one hundred shares. If you buy the shares, your downside risk is $1,541, with a potentially unlimited upside reward. Buying one protective put (to cover all one hundred shares) limits the amount you can lose, should the stock fall.

To see how this works, consider the following:

DOW trading @ $15.41		
Buy	100 DOW @ $15.41	$1,541
Buy	1 DOW MAR 15 Put @ $1.65	$165
Cost of Trade		**$1,706**

As a result of purchasing the put, the break even point in DOW stock is $1,706, or $17.06 per share. However, no matter how far the stock drops, as long as the put has not expired, the purchaser can always choose to exercise his put and sell shares at $15. This means the maximum amount at risk, is $2.06 per share, or thirteen percent. This is just slightly more than the price paid to purchase the put.

Maximum Profit: Unlimited.

Maximum Loss: Limited: Strike Price - (Stock Purchase Price + Premium Paid).

Maximum Loss: Limited to the premium paid for the put option plus the difference between the strike price and your purchase cost of the stock.

Maximum Gain: Unlimited as the stock can trade infinitely higher.

Upside Profit at Expiration: Gains in Underlying Share Value since Purchase - Premium Paid.

Break Even Point: Stock Purchase Price + Premium Paid.

If Volatility Increases: Positive Effect.

If Volatility Decreases: Negative Effect.

Selling Naked Put

Introduction

Naked options refer to the strategy of selling a Put without owning or shorting the stock. The term "Naked" is used because these are uncovered positions. The object of the strategy is to collect the option premium without ever having to buy the underlying stock. An investor will sell an Out-of-the-Money (OTM) Put against a security. The investor wants the option to remain OTM so it expires worthless and the investor will keep the premium. Naked Puts are a Bullish strategy.

Selling Puts is a common strategy. First, Puts are written when the market is expected to go up, and the market tends to go up historically more than decline. Secondly, writing a Put is sometimes used as a means of acquiring the underlying stock for less money. When an investor sells (shorts) a Put they are obligating themselves to have the stock Put to them at that strike price if the stock is trading below the strike at expiration. Generally, the stocks selected for selling Puts should be fundamentally sound and poised for growth. A Put seller should have the equivalent of the strike price in reserve, if it should be needed for stock purchase. All of the above discussion is without consideration of margin. Each brokerage firm may have different requirements on the cash needed for security. However, the use of margin just increases both the risk and potential reward. It is not recommended nor considered in this discussion.

Summary of Naked PUT Strategy

1. Write Puts only when you are bullish on the stock, index, or market in general.

2. Select candidates whose underlying stock is in an up-trend or has a recent BUY signal.

3. Select candidates whose fundamental outlook is positive and getting better.

4. Generally, the time to maturity should be no more than 2 to 3 months.

5. Diversify your Portfolio with 4 or more different stocks.

6. Out of the money options are most often selected since "in the money" options increase the probability of being exercised, even in a flat market.

These calculations were developed for those investors that use a naked option selling strategy. If you write naked Puts, these calculations help evaluate the return if the stock is not assigned to your account. It is assumed that the security for the transaction is cash and the amount of cash is the value of the strike price. For naked writing, the security is the cash in your account, required by your broker, to potentially purchase the contracted stock for the exercised option. Therefore, the strike price is the security required. This calculation is called "Percentage Yield Naked" and is basically the time premium divided by the strike price expressed as a percent.

Example

Goldman Sachs Group Inc. (GS) had a stock Price on December 31, 2008 of $84.39.

Sell 1 GS FEB 09 75 Put @ $4.70 = $470.00.

% Yield Naked = Time Premium ÷ Strike Price.

Breakeven at expiration: strike price – premium received.

Maximum profit: amount of premium received, occurs when the underlying stock price is above strike price causing the option to expire worthless.

Loss: Increases with fall in stock price, with the maximum loss occurring if the underlying stock were to go to $0. That would result in a loss equal to the strike price less the premium received.

Time decay will cause the option value to decrease as expiration nears.

Advantages

The strategy gives higher returns as you keep collateral in the margin account.

You can get the stock at a discounted price.

Chapter 6
Bearish Strategies

These strategies have been presented for academic reasons. This shall not constitute a recommendation of these strategies to any individual.

Long Naked Put

Introduction

Put buying (Long Puts) is considered to be speculative strategies by most investors. In a long strategy, an investor will pay a premium to purchase a contract giving them the right to "Put" the stock to someone (put). An investor who is long a naked put, meaning the investor does not own the underlying stock as in a married put, needs the underlying stock price to go down in order to gain a profit.

Advantages with Long Options

- Potential Profits can be quite significant when compared to the initial investment.
- Long Option positions are highly leveraged. Investors can control shares of a security for about 10 percent of the securities value.
- The maximum risk is the cost of the option.

Disadvantages with Long Options

- Long Options positions offer no downside protection, as one might have with a Covered Call trade, even though the maximum risk is low.
- Long Options are a depreciating asset. The value will always decrease as the expiration date is approached.
- Timing when entering a Long Option trade is critical as time is always working against the investor in this strategy.

Summary of the Long Put Strategy

1. Buy a Put only when you are extremely bearish on the stock, index, or market in general.
2. Buy a Put if you are looking to protect shares of stock you have purchased (Protective Put Strategy discussed earlier).
3. Select a candidate whose underlying stock is in a downtrend or has a recent SELL signal.
4. Investors may look to buy a Put 3 or more months out in time to give the stock time to move in the desired direction.
5. Conservative investors may buy an ITM (strike above the stock price) or ATM Put; speculative investors may buy OTM (strike below the stock price) hoping for a large return.
6. Potential profits are great, but the stock can only drop to $0.00, giving the Long Put its maximum value.

Example

Stock price of WMT closed at $54.68 on November 25, 2008.

Buy 1 contract of (WMT Jun 2009 55 Put) @ $8.25 = $825.00.

Total Cost = $825.

Break Even at expiration = Maximum Profit = Strike Price - Ask Price = $55 - $8.25 = $46.75.

Maximum Risk = Premium Paid = $8.25 per share, or $825.

As long as WMT is trading below $46.75 prior to expiration of the option, the position is profitable.

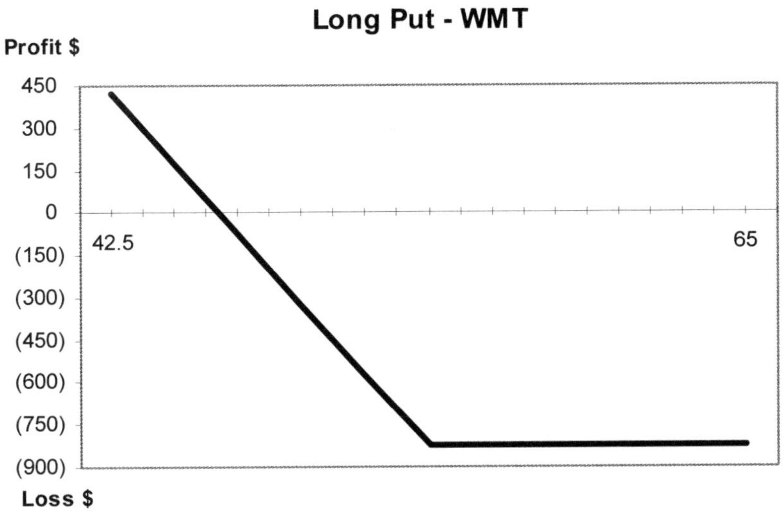

There are no return calculations for this strategy. Since there is no income received at the time of trade, a return on the investment can not be calculated until the position is closed. The return value is dependent on the stock price at expiration.

The return calculation at expiration would be:

[(Put Strike - Closing Stock Price) - Premium Paid] ÷ Premium Paid.

Assuming WMT were trading at $40 when the option expired, here is how we would calculate profit return:

[(55 - 40) - 8.25] ÷ 8.25 = 81.8% return on investment.

Married Call

Introduction

The Married Call strategy is the reverse of a Married Put strategy. In a Married Call strategy an investor will short (sell) shares of the underlying stock while purchasing a corresponding number of call contracts to protect the short position. The long call option, which is typically an OTM contract, serves as insurance for the short shares. It limits risk in the event the stock increases in value.

Because the investor is shorting (selling) stock, there is an overall net credit for the position. The total net credit is equal to the value of the short position minus the premium paid for the long call(s). The net credit is the maximum profit for the position, and is also the Break Even point for the underlying stock. The maximum profit could only be achieved if the stock were to go to $0, which is unusual but not impossible. Some profit can be realized if the stock is trading even slightly below the Break Even point. The maximum monetary value at risk is equal to the strike price of the protective call minus the net credit.

Investors use the Married Call strategy to protect the short shares of stock against a large gain in the underlying stock price. This is a bearish strategy, as the investor is looking for a decline in the underlying stock to earn a profit. The purchased call gives the investor insurance on the position, for an additional cost.

The value of the short position minus the cost of the call is the Net Credit.

The maximum risk is equal to the call strike price minus the Net Credit.

The maximum profit is equal to the Net Credit (if the stock drops to $0.00).

The Break Even point is equal to the Net Credit minus the call ask price.

Calculations for the Married Call Strategy can be understood with the following example.

You can enter into this trade by selling shares of Trimble Navigation Ltd. (TRMB) short, and buying equivalent number of call contracts against those shares sold.

Sell Short 100 Shares of TRMB @ $22.30 per share = ($2,230).

Buy 1 Contract of (TRMB May 2009 25 Call) @ $1.85 = $185.

Total value of your position will be equal to the value of short position minus the cost of calls. This will be your net credit.

Total Cost = - $2,045.00.

Net Credit = Short Stock Price - Call Ask Price.

Net Credit (Max Profit) = $22.30 - $1.85 = $20.45.

Break Even = Net Credit.

Break Even = $20.45.

Maximum Risk = Call Strike Price - Net Credit.

Maximum Risk = $25 - $20.45 = $4.55.

% Max Risk = Maximum Risk / Net Credit.

% Max Risk = $4.55 / $20.45 = 22.2%.

Profit is realized when the stock is trading below the Break Even point.

Maximum Profit = Net Credit (if stock is at $0.00).

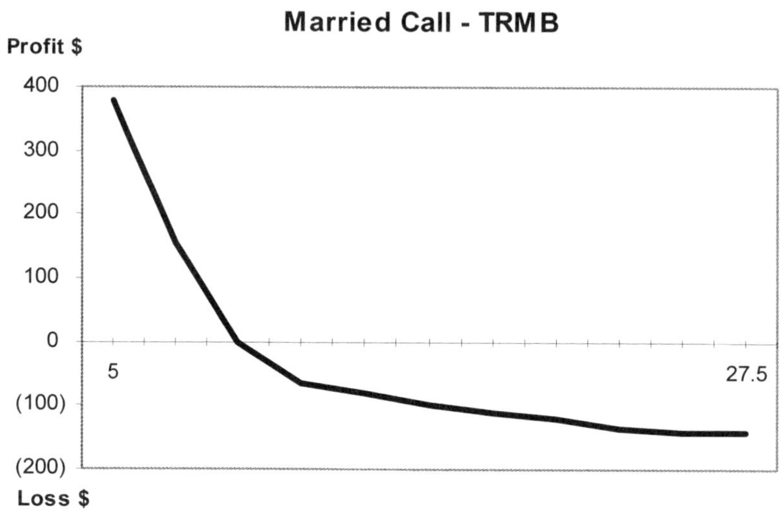

This example is OTM Married Call. By utilizing an OTM call, there is some additional risk, but significant higher break even is attained. The higher the break even price on any short, the greater the likelihood of profitability.

An in the money or at the money call can be used, but it would mean the break even point is lower. On a short position, a lower break even decreases the likelihood of profitability.

Advantages of this Strategy

Potential profits can be significant in a downward trending market.

The maximum loss is limited due to the protection of the call.

Married Calls allow investors to enter a short stock position with lower risk.

This strategy provides safety against a surprise gap up in the value of the stock due to an unexpected positive news announcement.

Disadvantages of this Strategy

The investor will have to pay an additional premium for the extra protection.

Although the strategy greatly reduces risk, it does not erase all risk.

Since an option is purchased, time works against the investor unless the stock moves down in value equal to the decay of time value.

Selling Covered Put

Introduction

The covered put strategy is just the opposite of the covered call strategy. You sell short the stock to cover the put that is written. The process to implement the covered put strategy is:

Short the stock.

Collect premium when writing the put.

Incur risk is if stock goes up (because of short).

If assigned utilize stock that is put to you to cover short position.

The covered put strategy is a neutral to bearish strategy because the investor is expecting the stock to go down or stay neutral. When the stock drops, the investor will have the stock put to them at the short put strike price. This "covers" the obligation of the shares of stock that were shorted. The investor keeps the initial premium received from selling the put. If the stock rises the investor keeps the premium, but is still holding the short stock obligation and could sustain a loss to close the short. If the short put does expire worthless without assignment, the investor could look to sell another put at a different strike for the next expiration month.

Example

Stock price of WMT closed at $54.68 on November 25, 2008.

Sell 1 contract of (WMT Jun 2009 55 Put) @ $8.25 = ($825.00).

Sell short 100 shares of WMT (Wal-Mart Stores Inc.) @ $54.68 = ($5,468.00).

Break Even = Short Stock Price + Option Cost = $62.93.

Maximum Profit = [(Short Stock Price - Strike Price) + Option Cost = $7.93.

% Downside Protection = Option Cost ÷ Short Stock Price = 15%.

% Return if maximum profit is realized = 12.6%.

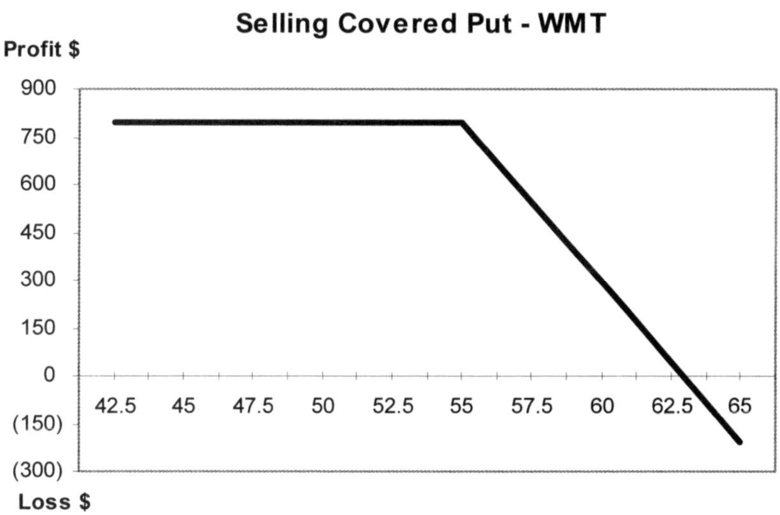

Cautions with this strategy

The Maximum Risk is infinite, as the stock can continue rising.

Most conservative investors shy away from shorting stock.

If good news comes out, the stock could rise suddenly, faster than the investor can roll the put, or close the position all together.

Most investors looking to collect premium trading puts will simply sell a Naked Put or trade a Bull Put Credit Spread.

Option Credit Spreads

A credit spread is established with all calls or all puts that have the same expiration date. A "credit" is put into a trader's account when an option is sold at a particular strike price which is closer to the current stock price of a security. The same number of option contracts is bought of the same security, with the same expiration month, but at a strike price further away to limit risk. The trader gets a credit initially because the option sold is more expensive option than the option purchased. The reason for this is simple. The option sold has a strike price closer to that of the current market price, making it more valuable. Remember that both the options should be of the same expiry date.

Credit spreads come in two types – the bear call spread and the bull put spread.

The Bear call option credit spread is a neutral / bearish directional spread used with call options (bear call) while bull put option credit is a neutral / bullish direction spread used with put options (bull put).

For example, XYZ stock is currently trading at $173. After reviewing the yearly price chart of XYZ stock and studying the other technical indicators, you felt confident that it will not only stay above $145, but it looks to trend even higher than the current price of $173. In order make money in this scenario, one would sell the 160 put simultaneously buy the 155 put as a single transaction. This transaction gives an up-front net credit of option premium. As long as the XYZ price does not go below the 160 level by expiration date, this trade would be a winning one as both options will expire worthless. The entire premium collected at the beginning will be retained by the trader.

One would take advantage of "time decay" by selling option credit spreads with a short time to expiration. The trader should create a credit spread with a maximum of 4–6 weeks to expiration. Sometimes they can be created with less than 2–3 weeks to expiry if you are certain of the short term direction of the underlying stock.

Option credit spreads enables the collection of income because due to its selling nature, but provides a cushion for directional error. This strategy also offers limited loss to the trader. This strategy can be used in any market situation, at any time and for any kind of security. With such plasticity and power of credit spreads, one can safely trade options. Of course, like all of the option strategies discussed in this book, they may not be appropriate for everyone.

Look at another example. In December, ABC stock is currently at $34 and you believe that over the course of the next month or so, you not only believe the stock will trend higher, but you also feel that the stock will not go below $30. You could trade a Bull Put Spread with January expiration. You would buy the January 25 put for $0.25 and you would sell the January 30 put for $1.00. This leaves you with a credit of $0.75, which of course equates to $75 per option contract you trade. The risk of the trade is $425 per contract. Assuming you are correct regarding the future trading pattern of ABC, you stand to make a return on investment of 17.5 percent in the time between now and January expiration.

There is another potential opportunity to realize a profit. At some point while the position is open, you might find the February 30 put trading at $0.90 and the January 25 put trading at $0.40 due to a change in the price of the underlying stock. If you buy the spread back, this would cost you $0.50 and the trade would be closed. This results in a gain of $0.25 ($0.75 - $0.50).

Bear Call Spread

Introduction

This strategy is to realize a profit by making cash that is a net credit formed by the difference in a Short Call price and a Long Call price. While the stock goes down, the investor keeps the net credit (difference in premiums).

- SELL a CALL at or out of the money (lower strike price).
- BUY a CALL one or more strikes above #1 CALL in the same month, this provides the upside safety.
- The margin requirement is the difference between the strike prices, usually 5 points/dollars.
- The maximum risk is the difference between the strike prices, less the net credit (difference in premiums).
- The maximum profit is the net credit (difference in premiums).
- The break even point is the lower strike price (#1) plus the net credit.
- Profit is realized when the stock price falls below this number.
- Maximum profit is made when the stock price falls below the lower strike price (#1 CALL) and remains there until expiration of the options.
- A profit is realized at any stock price between the break even point and the net credit.

The return calculations for the Bear-Call Credit Spread are:

% Return = (Premium on Short Call - Premium on Long Call) ÷ (Margin - Net Credit).

% Return = (Net Credit) ÷ (Margin - Net Credit).

Margin requirement = Short Call strike price - Long Call strike price.

Net Credit = Premium on Short Call - Premium on Long Call.

Example

Stock price of WMT closed at $54.68 on November 25, 2008.

Sell 1 contract of (WMT Jun 2009 55 Call) @ $7.45 = ($745.00).

Buy 1 contract of (WMT Jun 2009 57.5 Call) @ $6.40 = $640.00.

Total Cost = ($105.00).

% Return = (Premium on Short Call - Premium on Long Call) ÷ (Margin - Net Credit).

% Return = (7.45 – 6.40) ÷ [(57.50 - 50) - (7.45 – 6.40)] = 72.4% if stock is < $55.

Maximum Risk = Margin - Net Credit = $2.50 - $1.05 = $1.45, if stock is > $57.50.

% Maximum Risk = 100%.

Maximum Profit = Net Credit = $1.05, if stock is < $55.

Break Even = Lower Strike + Net Credit = $55 + $1.05 = $56.05.

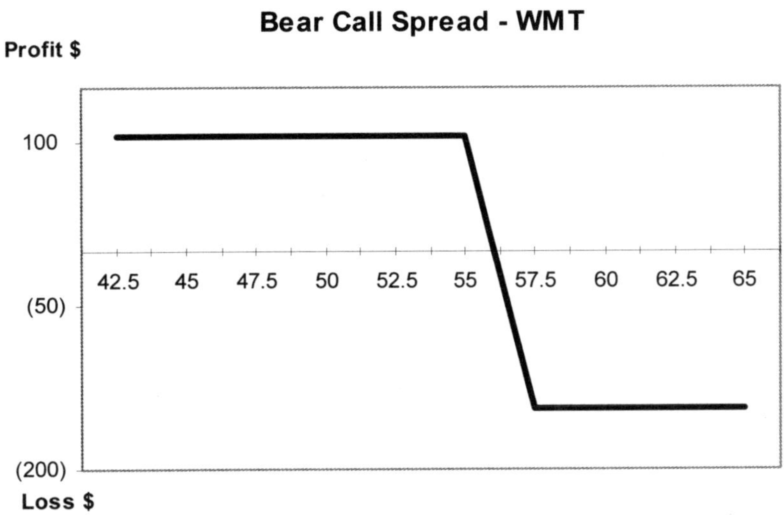

Advantages of this strategy

This is a BEARISH strategy; the profit can only be realized when the stock price falls from current price to a number below the break even price.

Losses are limited to the difference in strike prices, which is usually 5 points or less, minus the net credit.

Risk can be controlled by how far out of the money the sold option is positioned. Further OTM spreads will yield less profit, but are safer and have a higher break even point.

In the face of a rise the investor can buy back the Short Call and have unlimited profit potential from the Long Call.

The position is highly leveraged because of the low margin requirement on the spread.

This is an option only strategy; no shares of stock are actually owned (Uncovered / Naked position).

Cautions with this strategy

If the stock price falls very low, gains are limited to the net credit.

Anytime the underling stock/index price is above the short call strike price, there is a chance that you may have to deliver shares of stock to meet the short call obligation. If the underlying share price is between the two call prices, you may choose to buy shares of stock at the market price and then deliver them to the owner of the Short Call. If the stock is trading above both strike prices, you may realize the maximum loss on the position by exercising your long call and delivering those shares.

The credit you receive for the trade is generally much smaller than the max risk of the trade; therefore it is sometimes prudent to close the short option before the position is at max loss. Many traders do this when the short option is close to at-the-money.

If you have closed the short option half of the trade you may want to consider holding the long option to possibly profit from continued directional momentum in the underlying. However, the danger is that the underlying stock will correct and whipsaw in the other direction. If this were to happen, it is likely that the Long Call would then expire worthless.

Bear Put Debit

Introduction

This is a BEARISH strategy, where an investor will sell an At the Money (ATM) or slightly In the Money (ITM) PUT (creating a Short Put), and then buy a deeper ITM PUT (creating a Long Put). The PUT that is purchased is deeper ITM, resulting in a net debit.

BUY an ITM (In the Money) PUT.

SELL a PUT one or more strikes below the Long Put, but expiring in the same month.

The net investment or maximum risk is the net debit.

The maximum profit is realized if the underlying stock depreciates and is anywhere below the lowest strike price.

The break even point is the higher strike price (Long Put) minus the net debit.

Profit is realized when the stock price falls below the break even at or near expiration.

Maximum profit is made when the stock price falls below the lower strike price (Short Put).

Profit is achieved when both legs of the position are liquidated, prior to expiration. If both options expire worthless, it would result in a loss.

The return calculations for the Bear-Put Debit Spread are:

% Return = Maximum profit / Net Investment.

% Return = (Difference in strikes - Net Debit) / Net Debit.

Net Debit (out of pocket investment) = Premium on Long Put - Premium on Short Put.

Example

Stock price of WMT ended at $54.68 on November 25, 2008.

Sell 1 contract of (WMT Jun 2009 55 Put) @ $8.10 = ($810.00).

Buy 1 contract of (WMT Jun 2009 57.5 Put) @ $9.50 = $950.00.

% Return = (Difference in strikes - Net Debit) / Net Debit.

% Return = [57.50 - 55 - (9.50 – 8.10)] / (9.50 – 8.10) = 78.6%.

Max. Risk = Net Debit = 9.50 – 8.10 = $1.40, if the underlying stock is trading higher than $57.50 (both options would expire worthless and you would lose the entire Net Debit).

Max. Profit = Difference in strikes - Net Debit = (57.50 - 55 - (9.50 – 8.10)) = $1.10, if the underlying stock is trading lower than $55.

Break Even = Higher Strike - Net Debit = $57.50 – 1.40 = $56.10.

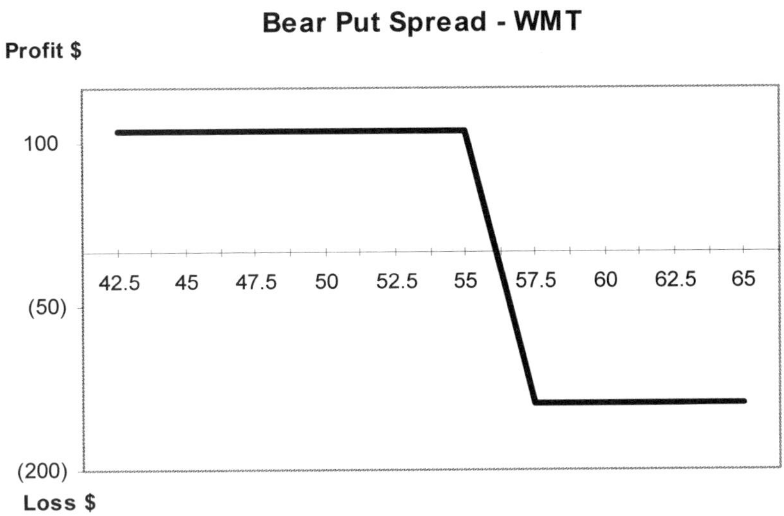

Advantages of this strategy

This is a BEARISH strategy; the profit can only be realized when the stock price falls from current price to a value below the break even point.

Losses are limited to the net debit.

No stock is actually owned (uncovered position).

In the money (ITM) puts offer high break even points (more safety), but more limited profits.

Out of the money puts offer larger profits, but have lower break even points, which require a fall in the price of the stock to realize gains.

Disadvantages of this strategy

When compared with a credit spread, an "out of pocket" investment is required.

If the stock prices were to go down considerably, gains are limited to the maximum profit above.

If the stock were the subject of a positive news announcement that caused a sharp move upward in the stock price, the options would likely expire worthless.

Calendar Put Spreads

Introduction

The Calendar Put Spread (Including LEAPS) is a bearish strategy. This strategy is the reverse of the Calendar Call Spread. In this strategy an investor will buy (long) an in-the-money put that typically has 6 months to 2 years before expiration, and sell (short) a near term put at a lower strike price. Because the Long Put is both in-the-money and has more time value, this strategy is always a debit transaction. A profit will be realized if the underlying stock moves below the break even point. Some investors will trade same strike Calendar Put Spreads (horizontal) which is a less conservative strategy than diagonal spreads.

- Buy an ITM put with a few months to a year or more in time value.
- Sell a near term put one or more strikes below the Long Put.
- The net investment is the net debit (difference in premiums).
- The maximum risk is the net debit (difference in premiums).
- The maximum profit is realized if the stock is anywhere below the Short Put strike (lower strike price) at expiration. The maximum profit is equal to the time value left in the Long Put at the sold option expiration minus the net debit.
- The break even point is the point at which the value of the Long Put will equal the net debit. A profit is realized at any price below the breakeven point.

The return calculations for the Calendar Put Spread are:

% if Assigned = Maximum Profit ÷ Net Debit.

% if Assigned = (Long Put Time Value - Net Debit) ÷ Net Debit.

% Downside Protection = Premium Income ÷ Buy Price of Long Contracts.

% Downside Protection = Short Put Bid ÷ Long Put Ask.

% If Unchanged = [Long Put Value (at short put expiration w/ current stock price) - Net Debit] ÷ Net Debit.

Example

PowerShares Deutsche Bank Commodity Index Tracking Fund (DBC) was $23.26 on November 26, 2008.

Buy 1 contract of (DBC Jan 2010 25 Put) @ $5.40 = $540.00.

Sell 1 contract of (DBC Apr 2009 20 Put) @ $1.05 = ($105.00).

Total Cost = $435.

Max. Risk = Net Debit = 5.40 – 1.05 = $4.35 (if stock is above $25 at JAN 2010 expiration).

Max. Profit = 237 (if stock is below $20.00).

% Return = 54.5%.

Long Put Value = Black-Scholes model would used to determine the value of the long put when the stock price is at the lower strike.

Break Even = Stock Price when long put value is equal to net debit = $24.14.

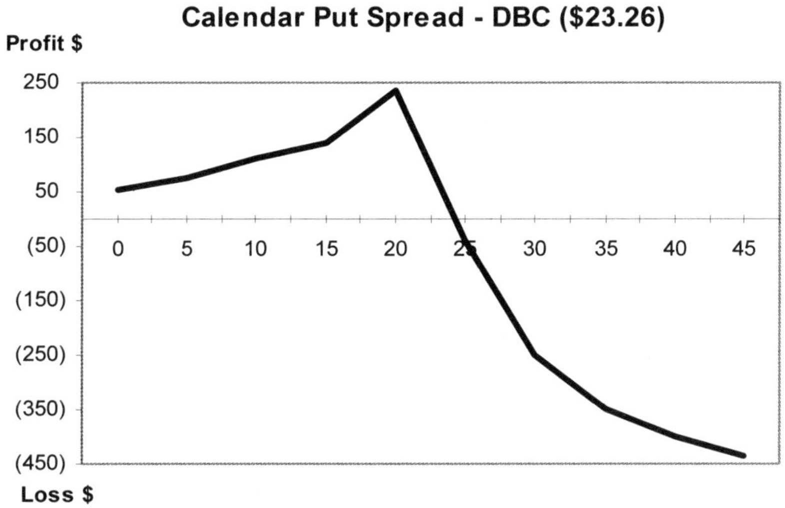

Advantages of this strategy

This is a BEARISH strategy, the profit can only be realized when the stock price is below the breakeven point.

Losses are limited to the Net Debit (Net Investment).

No stock is actually owned (uncovered position).

If an investor purchases the Long Put several months out in time, near term Puts can be written several times before the Long Put expiration. Therefore, the cost of the Long Put can be greatly reduced with many writes.

Cautions with this strategy

If the stock drops the gains are limited to the difference in the strikes minus the Net Debit.

If the stock drops very quickly there is the possibility of actually losing money if the near term put is assigned. Therefore, it is important that the difference in strike prices must be larger than the cost of the Long Put to assure a profit.

It may be difficult to write a near term Put for every write cycle (depending on the underlying stock options series).

In-the-Money Puts have a tendency to be assigned early. If the stock drops close to the Short Put strike price, you may want to roll out of the Short Put if you wish to avoid early assignment.

Selling Naked Call

Introduction

Naked option refers to the strategy of selling a Call or a Put without owning or shorting the stock. As outlined earlier, the term "Naked" is used because these are uncovered positions.

In a Naked Call trade an investor will sell a Call contract obligating them to deliver (sell) shares of stock at a set price. Selling Naked Calls is a Bearish strategy. As long as the stock remains below the strike price of the Call, the option expires worthless and the seller keeps the premium. The risk is if the stock goes up. The investor may be forced to buy shares of stock at a much higher price to deliver the stock at the lower strike for a substantial loss. The risk for the Naked Call trade is infinite, due to the fact that the stock could rise in price infinitely. Remember, this is a "Naked" option; the stock must be purchased at market price and delivered to the option buyer, in order to satisfy the CALL obligation if exercised. Because of this, Naked Calls are widely considered to be one of the strategies that carry the greatest inherent risk. Most brokerages will not approve the average trader to sell Naked Calls. In order to sell Naked Calls, an investor would have to demonstrate a substantial amount of sophistication, as well as assets.

The calculation for return for the naked "in the money" call is then based on the price of the underlying stock:

Example

DBC is trading at $23.26.

Sell 1 contract of (DBC Jul 2009 23 Call) @ $2.80 = ($280.00).

% Yield Naked (DBC Call) = Time Premium ÷ Stock Price 0.26 ÷ 23.26 = 1.12%.

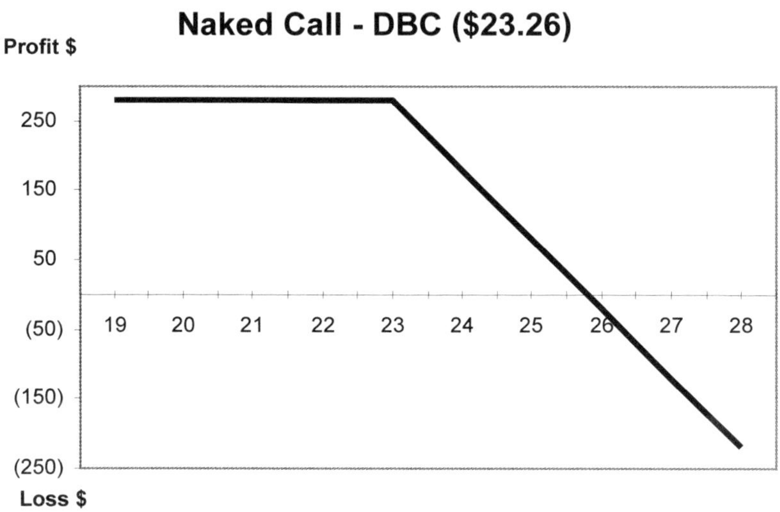

Typically, Naked Call writing is an "all or none" sort of trade. Either you will keep the entire premium because the call expired worthless, or you lose the initial premium received and more.

Look at this follow up to the above example:

Lets say that you wrote the Naked DBC (Jul 2009 23 Call) with 7 months until expiration. If the stock were to go to $30 per share with 4 months remaining until expiration that call would likely be trading at approximately $5.60. That would leave with only options.

You could do nothing and hope it comes back down by expiration. This means you not only risk the option being exercised, but you also would risk that the stock can continue trading higher.

Your other choice would be to close the position by buying back the call at approximately $5.60. This means that you not only lost the $2.80 you received in premium when you wrote the option, but you also now lost an additional $2.80 (multiplied by one hundred, of course) of your own money.

Even worse yet, imagine you wrote 10 calls, and the market price of DBC is $35! Needless to say, there is tremendous risk with Naked Calls. Although it can be a very lucrative strategy, make sure you fully understand your risk and potential loss before entering into this strategy!

Chapter 7

Neutral Strategies

These strategies have been presented for academic reasons. This shall not constitute a recommendation of this strategy to anyone.

Iron Butterfly Spread

Introduction

The Iron Butterfly is a neutral strategy similar to the Iron Condor. However, in the Iron Butterfly an investor will combine a Bear-Call Credit Spread and a Bull-Put Credit Spread setting the Short Put and the Short Call at the same strike price (At-the-Money). Due to the fact that the stock price rarely falls on an exact strike price, Iron Butterflies can be traded when the Short Call is slightly In-the-money (ITM) or the Short Put is slightly In-the-Money (ITM).

Once an investor has picked the strike price for the short options, the investor will look to purchase the same number of call(s) Out-of-the-Money (OTM) and the same number of put(s) Out-of-the-Money (OTM). The sold call(s) and put(s) make up the "Body" of the Iron Butterfly Position and the OTM purchased call(s) and put(s) make up the "Wings" of the position.

Since the investor is selling an ATM put and an ATM call, and then purchasing an OTM put and OTM call for protection, a net credit is achieved. Because there are two spreads in this position (four options) there is an upper and lower break even point. A profit will be achieved if the stock price is below the upper break even and above the lower break even. The maximum profit for the Iron Butterfly position occurs if the stock price expires right at the sold options strike price. All four options will expire worthless and the investor will keep the entire net credit. The maximum risk is equal to the differences in strike prices between the two calls or the two puts (whichever is greater) minus the initial net credit achieved.

In order to implement an Iron Butterfly, you would:

Identify a stock that you believe will not move very much, if at all. You must also identify a time period for which you believe the stock will remain at its current price.

Sell an equal number of At-the-Money put and call contracts with the same expiration month.

Buy the same number of put and call contracts one or more strikes Out-of-the-Money (OTM) in the same expiration month.

An overall net credit will be achieved. The net credit is the maximum profit. The maximum profit is realized if the stock is right at the short options strike price at expiration.

It is important to remember that there are 2 break even points, as profit is only realized if the stock is below the upper break even and above the lower break even.

The return calculations for the Iron Butterfly Spread are:

% Return = (Total Net Credit / Margin for the spread) x 100

Where:

Total Net Credit = Credit from Bull Put Spread + Credit from Bear Call Spread.

Margin = (Diff in strikes Bull-Put Spread OR Diff in Strikes Bear Call Spread Whichever is greater) – Net Credit.

Example

Stock price of Diamond Offshore Drilling Inc. (DO) was $76.98 on November 26, 2008.

Buy 1 contract of (DO Jun 2009 70 Put) @ $13.90 = $1,390.00.

Sell 1 contract of (DO Jun 2009 75 Put) @ $15.60 = ($1,560.00).

Sell 1 contract of (DO Jun 2009 75 Call) @ $15.90 = ($1,590.00).

Buy 1 contract of (DO Jun 2009 80 Call) @ $14.80 = $1,480.00.

Max. Profit = Net Credit = $15.90 + $15.60 - $13.90 - $14.80 = $2.80.

Max. Risk = Margin = Difference in Strikes - Net Credit = $5 - $2.80 = $2.20.

The upper break even for the position is equal to the short options strike price plus the total net credit.

Upper Break Even = Short Call Strike + Net Credit = $75 + $2.80= $77.80.

The lower break even is equal to the sold options strike price minus the total net credit.

Lower Break Even = Short Put Strike - Net Credit = $75 - $2.80 = $72.20.

Maximum Return = Net Credit ÷ Margin = $2.80 ÷ $2.20 = 127.2% (If DO is trading at $75 on expiration).

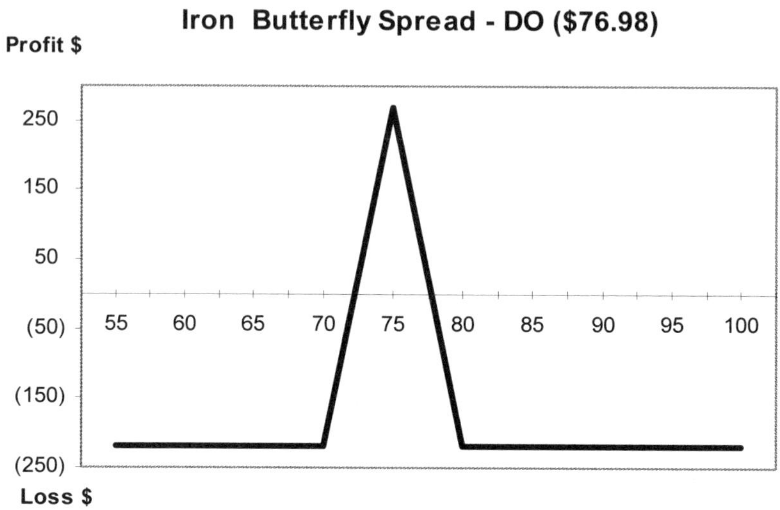

Advantages of this strategy

This is a NEUTRAL strategy. A profit can be realized anywhere below the upper break even and above the lower break even.

The double credit achieved helps lower the potential risk.

Potential returns are increased over a single Bear-Call or Bull-Put spread.

Losses are limited if the stock goes against you one way or the other.

If you are facing a large gain or drop in the underlying you could only close one leg of the four legs in the position.

No stock is actually owned (uncovered position).

Cautions with this strategy:

Commission costs to open the position are higher because there are four trades. Lower credit Iron Butterflies might be cost prohibitive due to large commission costs.

The maximum profit only occurs if the stock is at the strike price of the short option, at expiration.

Iron Butterflies offer a higher return then an Iron Condor spread, but they offer less safety. Due to the Upper and Lower Break Evens being so close to the current price of the underlying, the stock or index can only have a small movement before the Iron Butterfly trade is no longer profitable.

The credit you receive for the trade is generally much smaller than the max risk of the trade; therefore it is prudent to close the short option before the position is at max loss. Many traders do this when the short option is near-the-money.

If you have closed the short option half of the trade you may want to consider holding the long option to possibly profit from continued directional momentum in the underlying. If the stock were to climb or fall dramatically, you could still exercise or sell your In-the-Money long option to realize a profit.

Iron Condor Spread

Introduction

The Iron Condor Spread strategy is a neutral strategy similar to the Iron Butterfly. In the Iron Condor, an investor will combine a Bear-Call Credit Spread and a Bull-Put Credit Spread on the same underlying security. By doing this, an investor will potentially be able to double the credit obtained over a single spread position. Because there are two spreads involved in the strategy (four options), there is an upper break even and a lower break even. A profit is made if the stock remains above the lower break even point or below the upper break even point.

In order to implement an Iron Condor Spread, you would:

Enter a Bear-Call Credit Spread (Sell a Call at or out-of-the-money. Buy a Call one or more strikes above sold Call in the same target month).

Enter a Bull-Put Credit Spread in the same month, on the same stock (Sell a Put at or out-of-the-money. Buy a Put one or more strikes lower than short put in the same target month).

An investor will receive a net credit from both positions. The total net credit is the maximum profit. The maximum profit is earned if the stock price remains above the short put strike and below the short call strike.

The upper break even is the short call strike price plus the total net credit.

The lower break even is the short put strike price minus the total net credit.

A profit is realized at any price above the lower break even or below the upper break even.

The maximum risk is the difference in strike prices on either spread minus the net credit.

The return calculations for the Iron Condor Spread are:

% if Assigned = (Total Net Credit ÷ Margin for the spread) x 100.

Where Total Net Credit = Credit from Bull Put Spread + Credit from Bear Call Spread.

Margin = (Diff in Strikes Bull-Put Spread OR Diff in Strikes Bear-Call Spread whichever is greater) - Net Credit.

Example

Shares of Baidu, Inc. (BIDU) closed at $142.75 on November 26, 2008.

Buy 1 contract of (BIDU Jun 2009 120 Put) @ $29.30 = $2,930.00.

Sell 1 contract of (BIDU Jun 2009 130 Put) @ $31.70 = ($3,170.00).

Sell 1 contract of (BIDU Jun 2009 150 Call) @ $35.40 = ($3,540.00).

Buy 1 contract of (BIDU Jun 2009 160 Call) @ $34.20 = $3,420.00.

Total Net Credit = $3.60.

% Return = 22%.

Max. Profit = Total Net Credit = 3.60.

Max. Risk = (Maximum Difference in Strikes - Total Net Credit).

Max. Risk = 10 - 3.60 = 6.40.

Lower Break Even = Short Put Strike - Total Net Credit = 130 - 3.60 = $126.40.

Upper Break Even = Short Call Strike + Total Net Credit = 150 + 3.60 = $153.60.

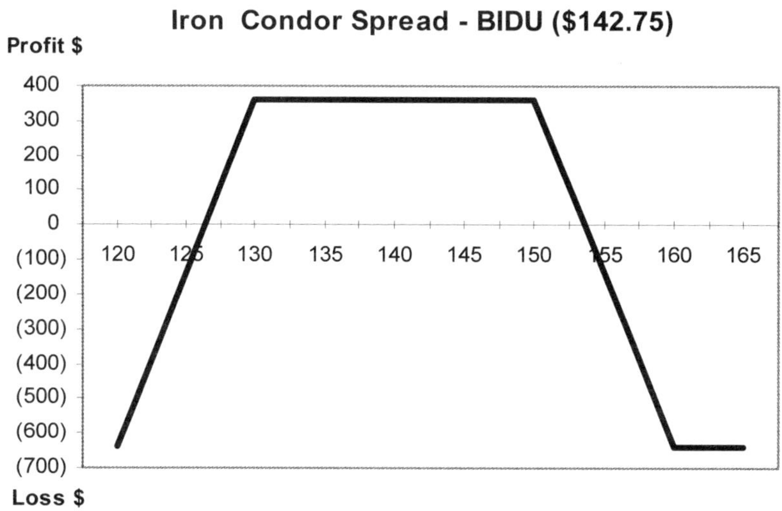

Advantages of this strategy

This is a NEUTRAL strategy. A profit can be realized anywhere above the lower break even and below the upper break even.

The double credit achieved helps lower the potential risk.

The risk can be controlled by setting your spreads further OTM.

Potential returns are increased over a single Bear-Call or Bull-Put spread.

Losses are limited if the stock goes against you one way or the other.

If you are facing a large gain or drop in the underlying you could only close one leg of the four legs in the position.

No stock is actually owned (uncovered position).

Cautions with this strategy

Commission costs to open the position are higher because there are four trades, and it might be cost prohibitive to trade iron condors that have lower net credits.

The credit you receive for the trade is generally much smaller than the max risk of the trade; therefore it is prudent to close the short option before the position is at max loss. Many traders do this when the short option is near-the-money.

If you have closed the short option half of the trade you may want to consider holding the long option to possibly profit from continued directional momentum in the underlying.

Long Straddle

Introduction

The long straddle position is when an investor purchases the same number of call and put options at the same strike price with the same expiration date. In this way, an investor can take advantage of any sudden movement in the stock price regardless of direction. This strategy might be employed shortly before an earnings announcement or an expected FDA approval notice is about to be in the news. The investor expects the stock price to significantly react to the news, but depending on the news event, the direction of the move is unknown. It is important to remember that volatility is necessary for a Long Straddle to be profitable. When selecting which security utilize in order to implement a Long Straddle, the stock should have a history of aggressive and significant short term moves in price. A sedentary or stagnant stock is not appropriate for this strategy. A stagnant security might be a candidate for the opposite type of trade, a Short Straddle, which is discussed in the next chapter.

As the investor is buying options there is a net debit to enter the trade. Typically, these strategies are implemented with options that have less than three months until expiration. This is due to the increased time value on the longer term options. The greater time value, the more volatile the stock needs to be in order to be profitable. The maximum risk in the position is equal to the net debit. By purchasing both a call and a put, there are both upper and lower break even points. A profit is realized on the position if the stock rises above the upper break even (possible unlimited profit potential) or below the lower break even (profit potential is limited to the difference between the lower break even point and zero).

Some investors also use a straddle play to take advantage of deflated option prices and low volatility. If both options are purchased at a discount, the investor assumes that volatility will rise to normal levels and theoretically, the price of both options may increase regardless of the stock price movement.

In order to implement a Long Straddle, you would:

Buy an equal number of calls and puts at the same strike price and expiration date.

The net investment is the net debit (total premiums paid).

The maximum risk is equal to the net debit (total premiums paid).

The position has both an upper break even and a lower break even.

Profit is realized if the stock goes above the upper break even or below the lower break even.

Calculations for Long Straddles are:

Upper Break Even = Strike Price + Net Debit.

Lower Break Even = Strike Price - Net Debit.

Probability Sum = (Prob. Above Upper Break Even) + (Prob. Below Lower Break Even).

Max Risk = Net Debit = Cost Of Position.

Where Net Debit = Premium of Bought Call + Premium of Bought Put.

Example

PowerShares NASDAQ 100 (QQQQ) was $31.33 on January 6, 2009.

Buy 1 contract of (QQQQ Feb 2009 31 Call) @ $1.79 = $179.00.

Buy 1 contract of (QQQQ Feb 2009 31 Put) @ $1.50 = $150.00.

Max. Risk = Net Debit = = $3.29.

Upper Break Even= Strike + Net Debit = $34.29.

Lower Break Even= Strike - Net Debit = $27.71.

Maximum Profit = Unlimited.

As long as QQQQ is trading above $34.29 or below $27.71 by expiration of the option, the position will be profitable.

Advantages of this strategy

An investor can profit from this position if the stock moves in either direction.

The potential profit on the upside is unlimited as the stock could go up infinitely.

The potential profit on the downside, though limited by the fact that the stock can only go to $0, can be very significant.

The max loss is limited to the original cost of the position.

If volatility is low at the time of purchase and volatility rises, both options could profit even without an appreciable change in the stock price.

No stock is actually owned (Uncovered position).

Cautions with this strategy

If the stock remains at the original stock price, both of the options will expire worthless and you will sustain the maximum loss (net debit).

If the stock rises above the strike price but remains below the upper break even or above the lower break even you will still incur a loss on the position.

If volatility falls for both or either option, the position could lose with or without a stock price swing.

Short Straddle

Introduction

The short straddle position is created when an investor sells the same number of call and put options at the same strike price and expiration date. This strategy is best used on sideways or stagnant stocks. Unlike the Long Straddle which takes advantage of stock moves in either direction, the short straddle strategy is dependent on the stock price staying at the set strike price of the options at expiration.

As the investor is selling options there is a net credit achieved once the trade is activated. The maximum profit in the position is equal to the net credit. By selling both a call and a put, there is both an upper break even point and a lower break even point. A profit is realized on the position if the stock stays between the upper and lower break even points.

In order to implement a Short Straddle, you must:

Sell an equal number of puts and calls at the same strike price and expiration date.

The max profit is the net credit (total premium received).

The position has both an upper break even and a lower break even.

Profit is realized if the stock stays between the upper and lower break even points.

The maximum risk is limited to the difference between the strike price and $0 on the put side only, but is infinite on the call side (same as a Naked Call)

Calculations for Short Straddles are:

Upper Break Even = Strike Price + Net Credit.

Lower Break Even = Strike Price - Net Credit.

Probability Sum = (Prob. above Upper Break Even) + (Prob. below Lower Break Even) (Reflects Probability that the spread will fail. Look for a lower Probability Sum).

Max Profit = Net Credit = Premium received.

Where Net Credit = Premium of Sold Call + Premium of Sold Put.

% Return = Net Credit ÷ (Option Strike Price + Highest Option Bid) - Net Credit.

Example

Helmerich & Payne Inc. (HP) closed at $26.51 on November 26, 2008.

Sell 1 contract of (HP Jun 2009 30 Call) @ $5.20 = ($520.00).

Sell 1 contract of (HP Jun 2009 30 Put) @ $8.50 = ($850.00).

Max. Profit = Net Credit = $13.70.

Upper Break Even = Strike + Net Credit = $43.70.

Lower Break Even = Strike - Net Credit = $16.30.

% Return = Net Credit ÷ (Option Strike Price + Highest Option Bid) - Net Credit.

% Return = 29.6%.

Maximum Risk = Unlimited.

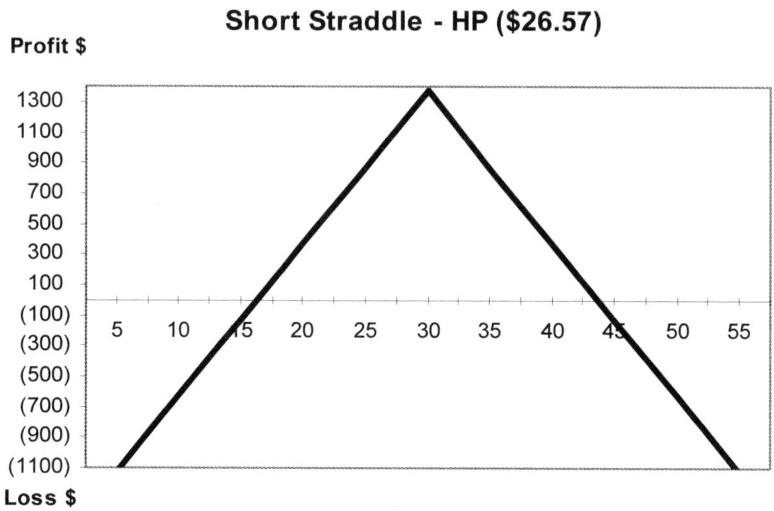

Advantages of this strategy

If the stock remains at the original stock price, both of the options will expire worthless and the investor will keep both premiums (maximum profit)

If the stock price remains below the strike price but above the lower break even point the investor will still realize a profit.

If the stock price remains above the strike price but below the upper break even point the investor will still realize a profit.

An initial credit is received on the transaction so the investor does not have to put up any money to enter into the position.

No stock is actually owned (Uncovered position).

Cautions with this strategy

The investor can take a loss if the stock swings quickly in one direction or the other due to unforeseen events.

The risk/max loss is infinite since the call portion of the trade is essentially a Naked Call.

Because of this risk, the margin requirements for this strategy are fairly high. Your broker may require you to cover both options as if they were two Naked Options, or they may require a cash value of the Option Strike Price plus the highest bid of the call or the put.

Long Strangle

Introduction

The Long Strangle position is similar to the Long Straddle strategy, except you purchase the call option(s) and the put option(s) at different strike prices. When entering a Long Strangle an investor will purchase an equal number of out-of-the-money (OTM) calls and puts for the same target month. Like the Long Straddle position, the Long Strangle has unlimited profit potential if the stock price moves enough in either direction.

As the investor is buying options there is a net debit to open the position. Because the purchased calls and purchased puts are OTM, the net debit is generally less for the Long Strangle than for a Long Straddle position. The maximum risk in the positions is equal to the net debit. By purchasing both a call and a put, there are both upper and lower break even points. A profit is realized on the position if the stock rises above the upper break even (unlimited profit potential) or falls below the lower break even (limited profit potential from the lower break even point to zero).

The Long Strangle is considered a neutral strategy as the investor stands to profit on the position from a movement in either direction. The investor is typically not concerned which direction the market heads, as long as the stock falls below the lower break even or rises above the upper break even.

To implement a Long Strangle, you would:

Buy equal number of out-of-the-money (OTM) calls and puts, all expiring in the same month.

The position has both an upper and lower break even.

Profits are realized if the stock rises above the upper break even or falls below the lower break even.

Example

Stock QQQQ at $29.31 on November 26, 2008.

Buy 1 contract of (QQQQ Feb 2009 33 Call) @ $0.79 = $79.00.

Buy 1 contract of (QQQQ Feb 2009 29 Put) @ $0.82 = $82.00.

Max. Loss = Net Debit (total premiums paid) = $1.61.

Upper Break Even = Call Strike + Net Debit = $34.61.

Lower Break Even = Put Strike - Net Debit = $27.39.

Calculations for Long Strangles are:

Probability Sum = (Prob. above Upper Break Even) + (Prob. below Lower Break Even).

Max Risk = Net Debit = Cost of Position.

Where Net Debit = Premium of Bought Call + Premium of Bought Put.

Advantages of this strategy

An investor can profit from this position if the stock moves in either direction.

The potential profits on the upside are unlimited.

The potential profits on the downside can be very high as well.

The max loss is limited to the original cost of the position (Net Debit)

There net debit is lower than the Long Straddle strategy.

Since both options are OTM, price decay on the options is not as rapid as they are with the Long Straddle.

No stock is actually owned (Uncovered position).

Cautions with this strategy

If the stock expires between the two option strike prices you will sustain the maximum loss (Net Debit).

If the stock rises above the call strike price but remains below the upper break even you will still incur a loss on the position.

Likewise, if the stock falls below the put strike price but remains above the lower break even you will still incur a loss on the position.

Since you are purchasing two different strikes you may need a large move in either direction to obtain a profit.

Short Strangle

Introduction

The Short Strangle strategy is similar to the Short Straddle strategy, except you sell the call option(s) and the put option(s) at different strike prices. When entering a Short Strangle position an investor will short an equal number of out-of-the-money (OTM) puts and calls for the same target month. Like the Short Straddle position, the Short Strangle position has a set maximum profit and potentially unlimited risk if the stock goes against you.

As the investor is selling options there is a net credit achieved when the position is opened. The maximum profit for the position is equal to the net credit. The maximum profit is realized if the stock remains stagnant and the stock price remains between the two strike prices at expiration. By selling both a call and a put there is both an upper and lower break even. Profit can be realized if the stock price is above the lower break even or below the upper break even at expiration. The stock can go infinitely higher, or fall to $0, resulting in potentially unlimited risk as the option(s) may need to be bought back to avoid assignment.

The Short Strangle is a neutral position. The investor will profit from the position if the stock stays stagnant and expires within the profitable range.

The maximum risk is infinite on the call side, as it is essentially a Naked Call, limited to the difference between the put strike price and $0 on the put side.

The position has both an upper break even and a lower break even.

Profit is realized if the stock price remains between the upper and lower break even points.

Calculations for Short Strangles are:

Probability Sum = (Prob. above Upper Break Even) + (Prob. below Lower Break Even) (Reflects Probability that the spread will fail. Look for a lower Probability Sum).

% Return = Net Credit ÷ (Call Strike Price + Put Premium) - Net Credit.

Example

Sell (short) out-of-the-money (OTM) call(s) in a particular target month.

Sell (short) the same number of out-of-the-money (OTM) put(s) for the same month.

HP closed at $26.51 on Nov 27th 2008.

Sell 1 contract of (HP Jun 2009 30 Call) @ $5.20 = ($520.00).

Sell 1 contract of (HP Jun 2009 25 Put) @ $5.70 = ($570.00).

Max. Profit = Net Credit (total premiums received) = $10.90.

Where Net Credit = Premium of Sold Call + Premium of Sold Put.

Upper Break Even = Call Strike + Net Credit = $40.90.

Lower Break Even = Put Strike - Net Credit = $14.10.

% Return = Net Credit ÷ (Call Strike Price + Put Premium) - Net Credit = 24.7%.

Maximum Risk = Unlimited.

Short Strangle - HP ($26.57)

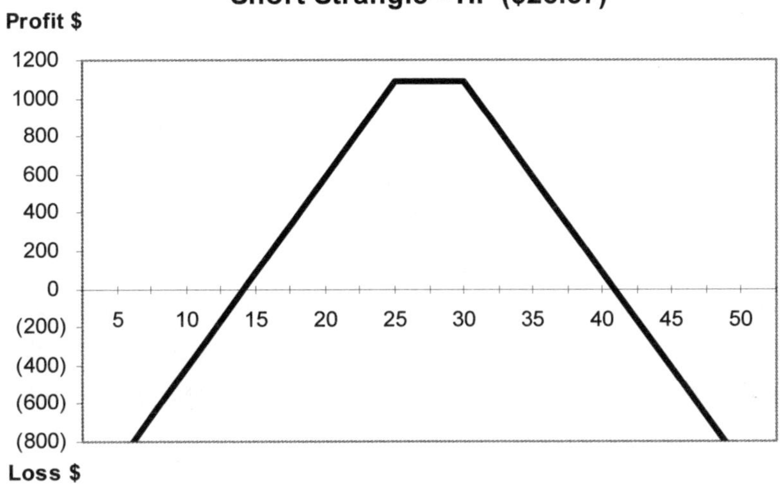

Advantages of this strategy

If the stock remains between both strike prices at expiration, both of the options will expire worthless and the investor will keep the entire Net Credit (maximum profit)

If the stock remains below the put strike price but above the lower break even the investor will still realize a profit.

If the stock remains above the call strike price but below the upper break even the investor will still realize a profit.

An initial net credit is received on the transaction so the investor does not have to put up any money to enter the position.

The investor is using two different OTM strike prices, and as a result the stock can move in a wider range than in the Short Straddle position and still be profitable.

No stock is actually owned (Uncovered position).

Cautions with this strategy

The investor can take a loss if the stock swings quickly in one direction or the other due to unforeseen events.

The risk/max loss can be almost infinite because of the obligation to buy or sell shares that are not owned.

Because of this risk, the margin requirements for this strategy are fairly high. Your broker may require you to cover both options as if they were two Naked Options, or they may require a cash value of the Option Strike Price plus the highest bid of the call or the put.

Because the investor is selling two OTM options, there is a lower net credit than with a Short Straddle position, but the stock has more space to move before the position is a loss.

Action must be taken if either of the options are ITM at expiration.

Chapter 8

Best Strategies

This chapter is a representation of the author's opinion. These strategies are suitable only for those who are experienced in trading options, and have the ability to undertake the risks associated with these strategies. Beginners must practice these strategies on paper before getting involved in actual trading. These strategies involve significant risk.

How to Pick the Best Stocks to Buy— 4 Simple Rules

Whether or not a stock is likely to move up is essentially to determining what, if any option strategies can be implemented utilizing it as the underlying stock.

Here are some of the criteria which may help you when making a decision whether or not you are selecting the stocks that have strong potential for increasing in value. It may not be possible to find many stocks which satisfy all of the following requirements. If you can satisfy 3 of the following 4 requisites, it may be worth giving some additional consideration.

1. Price of the stock divided by the book value should be less than 1.

Book value is the difference between values of assets and liabilities. Book value (BV) is the theoretical value of any share of stock. Simply put, if a company were to cease operations, sell all of its assets, and pay all of its liabilities, the amount remaining divided by the number of shares outstanding is the "book value". If we take the speculation out of the market, every stock should be trading at its book value. Both price and BV ratio measure amount paid for the shareholders equity. The lower the ratio of the stock price, to its book value, the greater the desirability of the stock. Although this calculation is readily available for stocks on most financial websites, you may calculate in this manner:

Price / Book ratio = market capitalization / book value of equity.

Price / Book ratio = (shares outstanding x market price of share) / (book value of assets minus liabilities).

This ratio is best used for companies that have significant assets. However, it can also be a valuable tool with smaller companies as well. Computing this ratio is simple and it is easy to understand. This provides quick view at how the market is valuing the company's assets and its earnings. This ratio is not influenced by accounting rules and hence the price to book value ratio works around the world.

However, the asset values are calculated using their purchase price, not the current market value. Hence the ratio may not give a precise measure. This ratio may be skewed somewhat for companies that rely on intellectual property. There is the chance that we may see an artificial lower P/B ratio when an acquisition takes place. Any recent write-offs will result in the reduction of the book value of equity.

2. P/E of the stock should be less than 70.

P/E is the ratio of the current price of the stock to the earnings of the last year. The higher this ratio is, more you are paying for the stock compared to its earnings.

P/E = Stock price / Earnings per Share.

It is used to determine how expensive or undervalued a stock may be against its earnings. The ratio gives an idea of the willingness of the market to pay for the company's earnings. Investors utilize this ratio to estimate if the stock is overvalued or undervalued. A lower P/E ratio may indicate that the stock is undervalued relative to its current earnings.

Some companies trade at higher P/E ratio when they are expected to grow exceptionally in the coming months or years. Sometimes a stock with a high P/E ratio can be a good investment, as the earnings may "catch up" to the price. Often times however, this does not occur. P/Es often can be inflated during market bubbles.

3. P/E/G of the stock should be less than 1

This is a comparison of a company's **P**rice/**E**arnings ratio to its earnings per share (EPS) **G**rowth. If we take speculation out of the market, P/E/G should be equal to 1. This would then verify that the company is "fairly valued". If P/E/G is less than 1, it means that the stock price is undervalued or that the company's future EPS growth will be lower than the market estimates. If it is greater than 1, it may mean that the stock is overvalued. The stocks with value tend to have P/E/G less than 1.

Many financial websites will also provide this ratio. However, it is calculated as follows:

PEG Ratio = (Stock Price / Earnings per share) / Projected annual earnings growth.

This ratio was developed to overcome the shortcomings in the usage of P/E ratio. The ratio is used to identify the undervalued or overvalued stocks using PEG ratios. Companies in different industries can have very different P/E ratios, but still be within an acceptable range. The P/E/G ratio provides a method to compare two companies to see which stock is the better investment.

The PEG ratio tends to work best with growth companies. This ratio figure is a rule of thumb, but by no means is it absolute. This ratio does not take inflation into account and it would be meaningless calculating PEG ratio if the rate of inflation is equal to that of growth rate. This ratio can be used as a supplement to other methods in order to come to a better conclusion.

4. Percentage of EPSG should be greater than 5 percent.

EPSG is the Earnings per share growth of the company. It is expressed as a percentage, and it symbolizes the expected earnings growth of the stock from one year to the next. The greater this percentage is more desirable the stock is.

How to Buy Stocks at Half-Price or Lower!

Please review the chapter "Why selling is key to success", before reading the suggestions in this chapter. This chapter is cantered on the thought of selling naked puts because that is the way to accumulate shares at prices below the current market price. Investor will have the choice between buying shares and writing those puts.

There is so much written against the idea of selling naked options that I dare to oppose it. Most brokerage companies discourage the idea of selling naked options. Why? I still have yet to find the answer to that question.

While I am opposed to the idea of selling naked calls, I am very much in favor of selling naked puts. If you sell a naked call, the stock may appreciate higher than you can imagine. Either you will end up buying the option back at a much higher premium or buying the stock at a much higher price, if the option gets exercised.

The reverse is true for the selling of put options. If you have decided to buy a certain stock at a certain price, why not consider buying it at half that price or less? Earlier in the book, I discussed that the stock market, in a short run has no logic. It is driven by the forces of supply and demand, which are influenced by greed and fear.

Let me explain using a simple example. Let us imagine that a stock is trading at $5. Its January 2009 put, with a strike price of 2.5, is trading at $0.50. The stock goes down to $1.50 on the 3rd Friday of January, 2009. You will be exercised on your put. This will result in you buying the stock at $2.50. Now the stock will cost you

$2.00 ($2.50 - $0.50). Remember, this was the stock that you intended to buy at $5.00, but now you bought it for $2.00. The worst that can happen is that the stock will go to absolute zero. Therefore, the most you can lose is $2.00 per share, which equates to $200 for a single option.

It is quite possible that the stock may start going up from $5.00 and you may never be able to buy the stock at a reduced price. However, if you had sold puts for different stocks, you may end up buying one of the other stocks at half price or lower.

Hence, one major difference between Naked Puts and Naked Calls exists. It is control after a losing trade. Having a Naked Put exercised will result in you owning stock. This gives you the potential to make back your loss on the option trade by the potential appreciation of the resulting long stock position. When a Naked Call is exercised, you purchase the securities in the open market and deliver them. There is no further opportunity to recapture money. However, it is important to remember that the long stock position that results from an exercised Naked Put can also depreciate resulting in additional losses.

When choosing to sell naked puts, select the stocks and strike prices with the following in mind:

1. Sell the puts as close to the $2.50 strike price as possible so your downside risk is limited.
2. Never sell more puts equal to more shares than you would be willing to own. If you are only willing to own 200 shares of a stock, do not sell more than 2 puts.

Naked Put Spreads										
	Stock	Price Change	Book	PE	EPSG	52 wk	Strike	Put	Put	Industy
Sym	Price		Value	Ratio	%	Range	Price	Bid	Bid	Kind
ABK	8.82	0.3	6.78		-113%	1.04 - 73.2	2.5		0.65	Insurance
CORS	5.1	0.31	13.42	11.59	-142%	2.2 - 16.1	2.5	0.65	0.55	Regional - Midwest Banks
GGC	4.56	0.06	3.22		-88%	1.96 - 15.71	2.5		0.4	Synthetic Materials

Example

Based on the spread sheet above, let us do some analysis for selling puts.

Here are some examples of buying stocks at half price or lower:

ABK—Sell a January 2010 2.5 put at $0.65. The stock is trading at 8.82. In the worst case scenario, you will end up buying the stock at 1.85 ($2.50- $0.65). If you end up buying the stock which is trading at $8.82 for $1.85, you are buying at a discount of 79 percent. Of course, it would take a tremendous fall in the stock price for the $2.50 put to be exercised, so unless this option had significant time until expiration, this option will likely expire worthless. That of course means you get to keep the premium. That make you a winner wither way.

CORS—Sell a January 2010 2.5 put at $0.55. The stock was trading at $5.10. If the stock were to trade at $2.20 (which is the 52 week low in this example) at the expiration, you can close the Short Put by buying back, or accept the stock received from the put being exercised. If the put is exercised, you are buying stock for $2.50 per share, which you considered buying at $5.10. The net price you would be paying would come to $1.95 (2.50 – 0.55). You end up buying the stock at $1.95 resulting in a discount of 62 percent from where you first considered purchasing the stock.

GGC—Sell a January 2010 2.5 put at $0.40. The stock is trading at $4.56.If the stock is trading at $1.96 (which is 52 week low) at the expiration, close the Short Put by buying back, or accept the stock received from the put being exercised. If the put is exercised, you then own shares of the company you considered paying

$4.56 for at a lower cost of $2.10. The net price you would be paying would come to $2.10 (2.50 – 0.40). You end up getting a discount of 54 percent from where you originally considered the position.

How to Get Paid While Waiting to Buy Stocks at Half-Price or Lower!

In the above strategy, it is quite likely that the stock prices may never end up going down below the strike price. In that case you may never end up buying the stock. But here is the advantage. The stocks never came down but the put options that you had sold will expire worthless. Therefore, you will end up making money while you were waiting for the stock to go down.

We will calculate the percentage return on the investment, for waiting for the stock to go down.

Beazer Homes Inc. (BZH)—Sell a January 2010 2.5 put at $0.45 while the stock is trading at $8.92. If you end up buying the stock, it will be at $2.05 ($2.50 - $0.45). That represents a discount of 77 percent.

BZH – Margin requirement = $70.

You profit if the price stays above $2.50, the put would expire worthless and as a result, you retain the initial premium received of $45.

The break even point is $2.05. If stock at that price were put to you at $2.50, and you sold it immediately for the market price of $2.05, the net result would be $0 once the original option premium were included.

MF Global Ltd (MF)—Sell a January 2010 2.50 put at $0.55 while the stock was trading at $7.33. The net price you would be paying would come to $1.95 (2.50 –

0.55). You end up buying the stock at $1.95 where you would get a discount of 73 percent.

MF – Margin requirement = $80.

You profit if the price goes higher because you will retain the initial premium received of $55. This is the premium you received to sell the put.

You profit if the price stays above $2.20. In the worst case you end up buying stock at $2.50 on which you already received a premium of $0.55. The net result is $1.95 ($2.50 - $0.55).

How to Make Money if the Stocks Don't Move Much Either Way!

There are two strategies to make money if the stocks don't move much in either direction.

Bull Put Credit Options													
Contract	Stock	Price/ Change	Strike	Bid	Strike	Ask	Net Cr	Range	BEP	BV	Price / Book	H. Vol	Industry
09 JAN	QID	47.87 (+0.57)	47	5.7	42	3.3	2.4	33.80 to	44.6		0	0.41	Inverse Broad Index
09 JAN	ITMN	18.21 (-0.32)	17.5	5.2	12.5	2.9	2.3	11.72 to	15.2	(2.07)	-8.78	0.46	Drug Manufacturers - Other
09 JAN	SRS	78.18 (-7.83)	75	10	70	8	2.2	78.80 to	72.8		0	0.89	Inverse Real Estate

1. Bull Put Credit Spread

Earlier in the book, it was discussed that Bull Put (Credit) Spreads are a low downside risk and limited reward strategy if the stock price is expected to go up or remain flat. Bull Credit Spreads are very similar to a naked put. The only difference is that the option is bought further out of the money, which protects the investor from a catastrophic event. A Bull Put Spread is implemented by selling a put option contract on a particular stock at a certain strike price (at or near money) and the same number of put contracts are bought on the same stock with the same expiration date, but with a slightly lower strike price than that of the Short Put. This transaction results in a net credit. This net credit will be maximum profit for the investor. Maximum profit is made when the stock price rises above the strike price at which put option is sold. Although bull put spreads are generally "out of the money" trades, they can also be put on "at the money" or "in the money", however, it will increases risk and potential profits.

The margin required to trade in bull put spreads is the difference between the two strike prices, multiplied by number of option contracts, multiplied by one hundred.

Margin = (sold put strike price x100) – (bought put strike price x 100).

Net Credit = premium on sold put – premium on bought put.

Cash required = [(higher strike price) – (lower strike price)] x number of contracts x 100.

% of profit = Net Credit / (margin-net credit).

The premium received at the time the trade is implemented will be applied towards the margin requirement. The breakeven point can be calculated by subtracting the net credit from the higher of the two strike prices. This is a good to implement if someone is unsure of the bullish expectations, but wants to participate in the stock. One can use this strategy when a rise in the underlying asset is expected, while still providing protection and profit if the underlying asset remains stagnant.

Examples

ProShares Ultrashort Nasdaq 100 (QID) is trading at 47.87. You could buy a put with a strike price of 42 for $3.30 and sell put with a strike price 47 for $5.70. You would receive a net credit of $2.40.

As long as the stock closes above 47; you will be able to keep the entire premium of $2.40. If it were to close below 47, you will start giving away the credit of $2.40 point by point. The break even point is $44.60 ($47 - $2.40). If the stock closes below $44.60, you have then exhausted the premium received, and you begin to incur losses.

Because you are long a put with a strike of 42, the maximum loss would occur if the stock were to close at or below $42.00. If you are still bullish about the stock after the option expires in January 2009, you can sell a January 2009 put with a strike price of 42. The option would likely be exercised resulting in you owning the stock with a cost to you of $42.00 per share, less the option premium received when you sold the put.

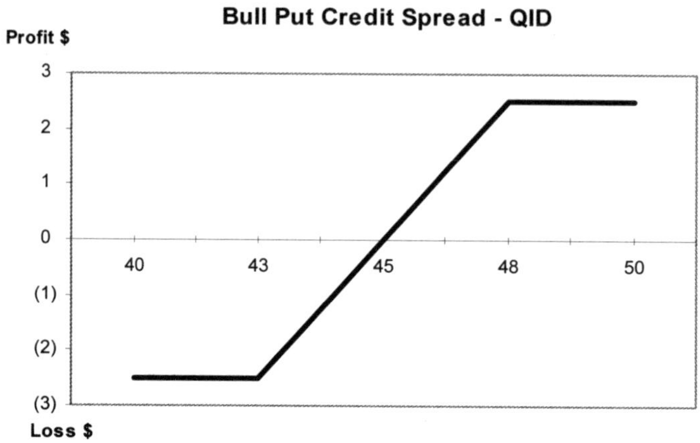

ITMN stock is trading at $18.21. You could buy a put with a strike price of 17.50 for $5.20 and sell put at strike price 12.50 for $2.90. You get a net credit of $2.30. As long as the stock closes above 17.50; you will be able to keep the entire premium of $2.30. But if the stock closes below $17.50, you will start giving away the net credit of $2.30. The break even point is $15.20 ($17.50 - $2.30). If the stock closes below $15.20, you will start to incur losses. The maximum loss of $2.70 would if the stock closes at or below $12.50. If you are still bullish about the stock after the option expires in January 2009, you can sell Jan 09 put at strike price $12.50 and upon exercise, you end up owning the stock at $12.50 less the put premium.

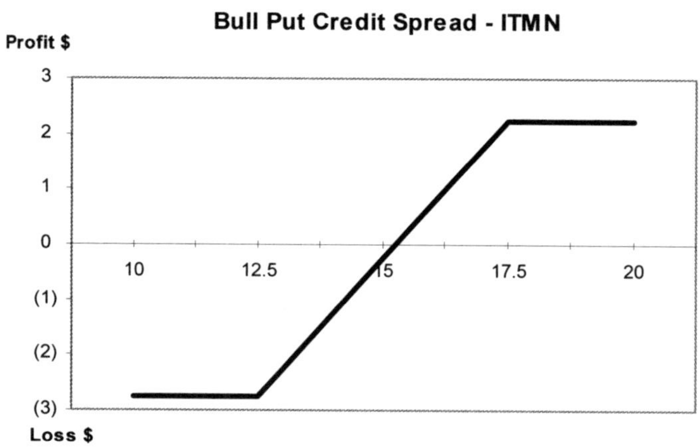

What makes this such a useful strategy is that risk is limited. However, your potential profits are also limited. The breakeven point, which of course is the difference between the higher strike price and the net credit, is quite possibly the most important component of this or any strategy. In this strategy, volatility is the enemy. You have to be confident the underlying will not suffer depreciation to a point lower than the break even. .

2. Bear Call Credit Spread

This spread is similar to bull put credit spread except it is used when you expect the stock to remain at about the same level, go up slightly or go down a lot. The spread involves buying a call (OTM) at a higher strike price and selling a call at a lower strike price (ITM) with the same expiration date. This strategy is considered to be a low risk and low reward strategy. The risk is minimized with the purchase of low priced call, which gives protection against an unexpected appreciation in the stock price. Profit potential is limited because the premium collected less the cost of the premium paid will be is the maximum profit.

In a bear market, the investor likely needs to follow a stock's trading plan using different analysis, strategies and trading tools. A bear call spread is one of the techniques where investor can try to find profits in a bearish market. One can make money by implementing this strategy, as long as the option does not go in the money (ITM) prior to expiration. As with any credit spread, the aim is to have the options expire worth less, meaning one can keep the premium received. The higher strike price acts as an insurance agent and the strategy can be more effective in declining or stagnant markets.

Bear Call Credit

Contract	Stock	Price/ Change	Strike	Bid	Strike	Ask	Net Cr	Range	BEP	BV	Pr/ Book	H. Vol	Industry
09 MAR	PAET	3.59 (+0.13)	2.5	1.3	5	0.4	0.5	2.45 to	3 - 7	4.662	0.77	1.2	Telecom Services - Domestic
09 MAR	TOMO	6.25 (+0.09)	5	1.6	7.5	0.75	0.05	4.63 to	5.05 -	4.735	1.32	1.09	Medical Appliances & Equipment
10 JAN	TRID	3.05 (-0.06)	2.5	1.1	5	0.45	0.15	2.76 to	2.65 -	3.91	0.78	1.25	Semiconductor - Specialized

Paetec Holding Corp. (PAET) stock is trading at $3.59. You could buy a Call with a strike price of 5 for $0.40 and sell another call at a strike price of 2.5 for $1.30. You receive a net credit of $0.90. As long as the stock closes below $2.50, both the calls will expire worthless and you will be able to keep the entire premium of $0.90. But if the stock closes above $5, you will lose $1.60 ($2.50 - $0.90), which is your maximum risk. The break even point is $3.40 ($5.00 - $1.60). If the stock closes above $5.0, you will begin to lose money. The maximum loss would occur if the stock closes at or above $5.

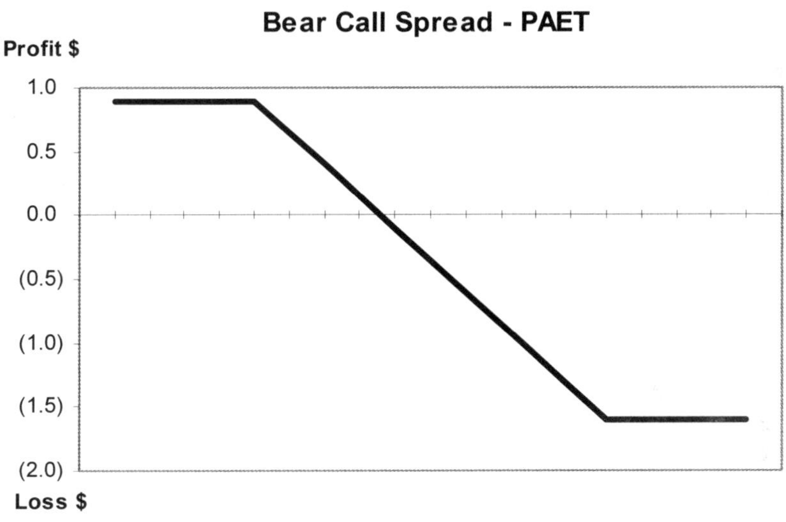

TomoTherapy Inc. (TOMO) stock is trading at $6.25. You could buy Call with a strike price 7.5 for $0.75, and sell another call with a strike price 5 for $1.55. You receive a net credit of $0.80. As long as the stock closes below $5, both of the calls will expire worthless and you will be able to keep the entire premium of $0.80. But if the stock closes above $7.50, you will lose $1.70 ($2.50 - $0.80), which is your maximum risk. The break even point is $3.30 ($7.50 - $4.20). If the stock closes above $7.50, you begin to lose money. The maximum would be realized if the stock were to close at or above $7.50.

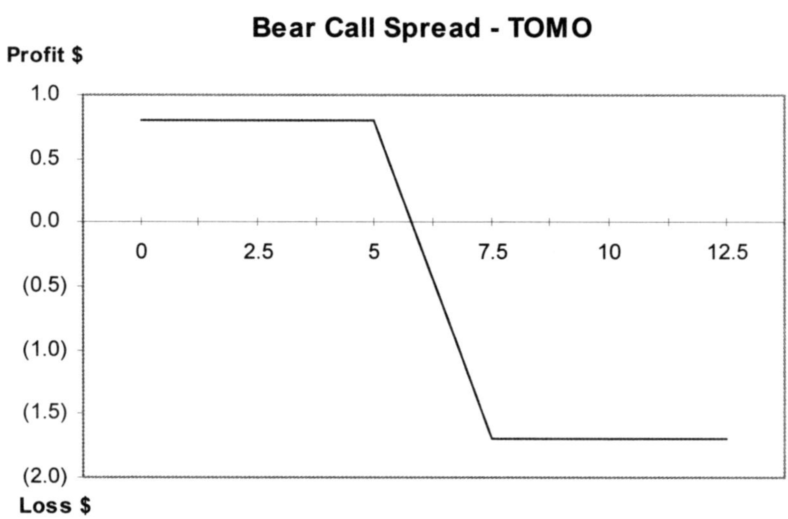

Trident Microsystems Inc. (TRID) stock is trading at $3.05. You could buy a call with a strike price of 5 for $0.45, and sell another call with a strike price of 2.5 for $1.05. You receive a net credit of $0.60. As long as the stock closes below $2.50, both the calls will expire worthless and you will be able to keep the entire premium of $0.60. But if the stock closes above $5, you will lose $1.90 ($2.5 - $0.60), which is your maximum risk. The break even point is $3.60 ($5.00 - $1.90). If the stock closes above $5.00, you begin to lose money. The maximum loss would be realized if the stock closes at or above $5.00.

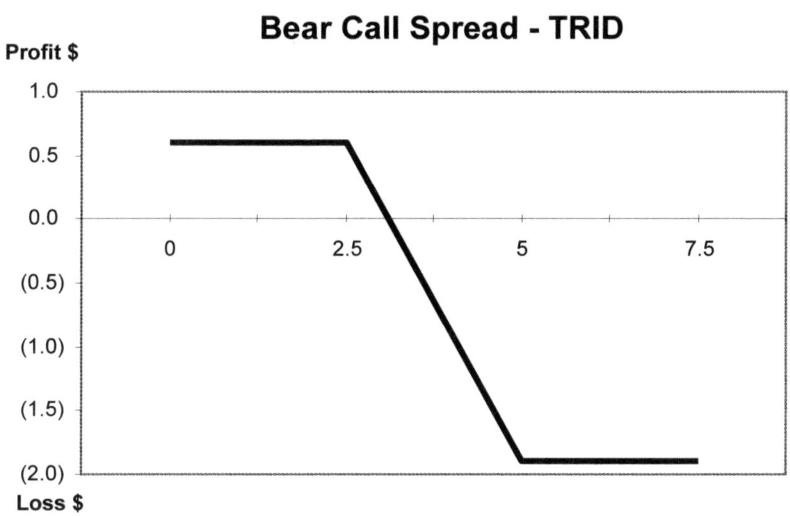

How to Make Money Whether Stocks Go Up or Down!

This strategy is most useful when the market is extremely volatile and if you are expecting a big movement in stock in either direction.

Sell a call at a strike price close to the trading price of the stock. Buy double or more the amount of sol calls. The long calls should be out of money at one strike price higher than the one which is sold. Do not overbuy the calls, as the net result should be a credit. All of the options should be expiring in the same month and they should have considerable time until expiration. The net result of this strategy is that you have more long calls than short calls. This means the net result would be positive if the stock moves strongly upwards. However if the stock does not move upwards or it moves downwards, it is still OK so far it makes a strong downward movement. A significant downward price move would mean all of the calls expire worthless, and your profit is the original net credit.

If the stock closes somewhere between the strikes prices of the long call and the short calls, you tend to lose money. The amount of the money lost shall be dependent upon the closing price of the stock. If the expected move in the stock price does not occur, both the positions can of course be closed. One of the biggest advantages of this strategy is that the time decaying factor of long positions reduced.

Nortel Networks Corp. (NT) stock is trading at $5.60. You could sell 1 call with a strike price 2.5 for $3. Buy 2 calls with a strike price 5 at $1.15. You receive a net credit of $0.70. Now you tend to lose money only when the stock closes between

$3.3 and $6.8. You tend to gain a lot when the stock goes above $6.8 because you have 2 long calls and only one short call.

Maximum Loss = $1.76.

Maximum Profit = Unlimited.

Total Cost = $ 0.70.

NT has a 52 week trading range of $5.51 to $19.50. There is the possibility of the price going up as it is currently trading near fifty two week low. However, as with any stock, there is always the potential that the stock could make new lows. With strategy, you can benefit regardless of the direction that the stock heads in, as long as the move is significant enough.

PROFIT & LOSS (at expiration) TABLE								
2.4	3.2	4	4.8	5.6	6.4	7.2	8	8.8
70	0	-80	-160	-120	-40	40	120	200

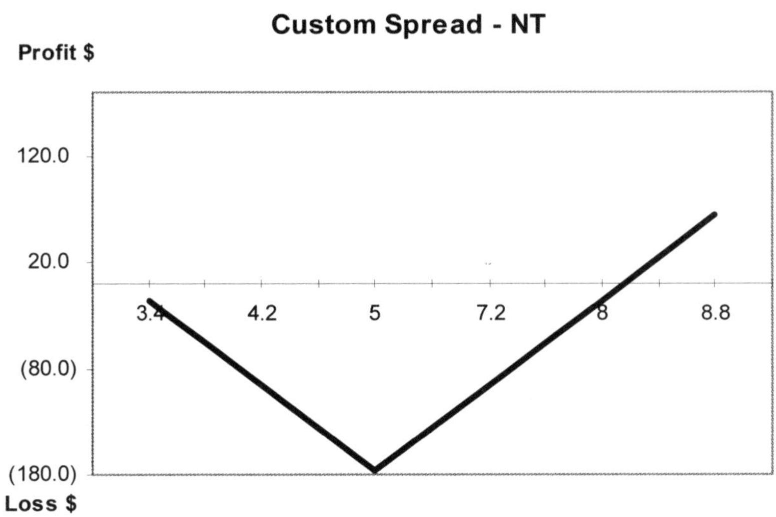

Stillwater Mining Co. (SWC) stock was trading at $6.65 on September 8, 2008. You could sell 1 call with a strike price of 5 for $2.15, and buy 2 calls with a strike price of 7.5 at $1.05. You receive a net credit of $0.05. Now you would likely lose money only when the stock closes between $5.05 and $9.95. You gains would be greater if the stock goes above $9.95 because you have 2 long calls and one short call.

Total Cost = ($0.05).

The 52 week trading range of SWC is $6.14 to $22.72, meaning that this stock is also trading closer to the low.

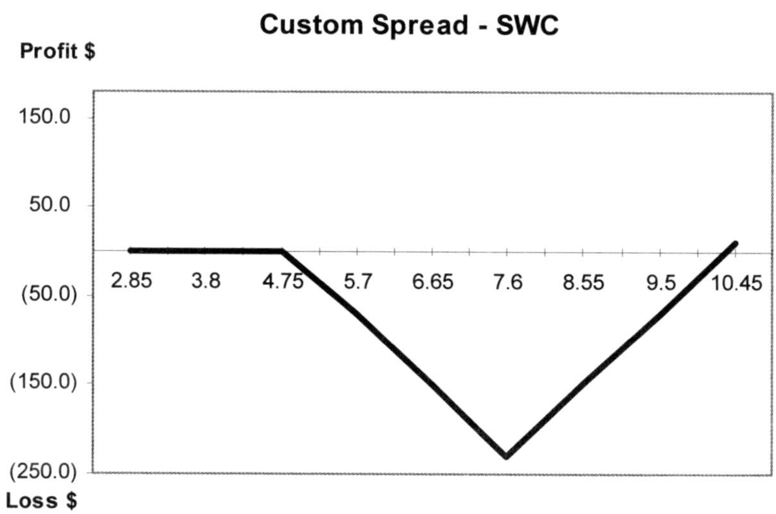

If you feel the stock is more likely to move downward in price, the same strategy can be implemented using puts. Simply sell 1 put in the money and buy 2 or more puts out of the money.

Titanium Metals Corp. (TIE) stock was trading at $8.03 on January 9, 2009. You could sell 1 June 2009 7.50 put for $1.55 and buy 2 June 2009 5.00 puts for $0.60. The resulting net credit is $0.35. As long as the stock is above $7.15, or below

$4.65, the position is profitable. If the stock were to trade in a range that is between the two strike prices, the result would be a loss.

GTX Inc. (GTXI) was trading at $13.31 at the close of the market on December 1, 2008. You could sell 1 put with a strike price of 12.50 for $2.05 and buy 2 puts with a strike price of 10 at $0.40. The resulting net credit is $1.25. You would suffer a loss only when the stock closes on expiry date (February 21, 2009) between $8.75 and $11.25.

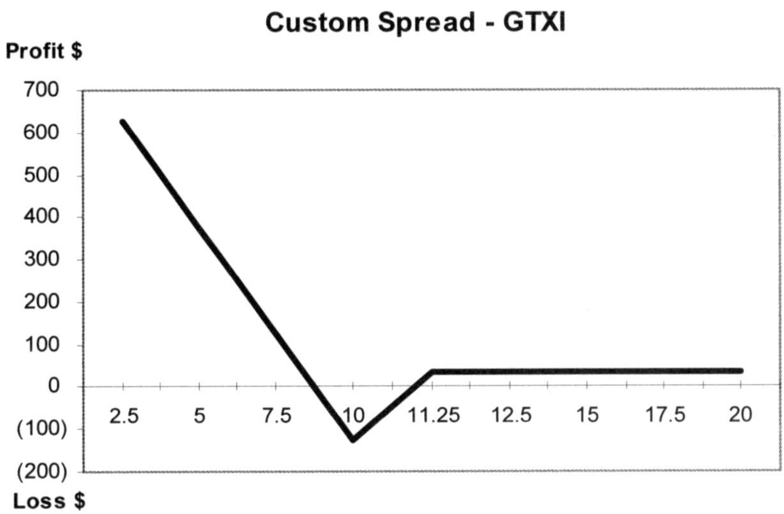

Selling Covered Call

The covered call strategy is straightforward. Monthly cash income is generated by selling call options against stock that you own. When selling a call option you are contracted to deliver your long stock at the strike price at any time until the option expires. In other words, the buyer has the right to buy your stock (at the strike price), and you are paid a premium (price paid for the purchase right). This investment strategy works well in a rising market. Why? It helps to maximize the yield (premium) of the long stock. What is safe about this strategy is that it works well in a declining market, also. How? Use of this strategy can minimize losses by offsetting your stock's devaluation with premium income. If you plan to hold the stock you buy or own for a long period of time, then writing covered calls (selling call options on owned stock) can greatly enhance the yield performance of your stock portfolio.

Call options can be written monthly on the stocks you own. This is because the highest premiums are realized over single month periods, rather than two or more months out in time. The stocks you choose to hold or buy should be stocks you would not mind owning for a long period of time. They should be steady growth stocks that have done well over the long term and can be prudently held even if a market decline occurs.

To keep commissions down, it's best to write calls in contracts (lots) of five to ten. Each contract represents one hundred shares, so plan to hold five hundred to one thousand shares of each stock. It is also desirable to have a least six or more stocks in your portfolio. It is important to implement diversity (selecting stocks from different industries and sectors) when selecting these companies.

In general, the stocks you wish to write a covered call on should be priced between $10 and $30 per share. This price range makes the yield higher. Because the call premium (money received for sale of the option) does not go down as fast as the stock price, a higher yield is usually obtained with lower-priced stocks.[2]

Example

The share price of Alexion Pharmaceuticals, Inc. (ALXN) is $31.00 on November 21, 2008.

Sell 1 contract of (ALXN May 2009 30 Call) @ $9.10 = ($910.00).

Buy 100 shares of ALXN (Alexion Pharma. Inc.) @ $31.00 = $3,100.00.

Total Cost = $2,190.

Maximum Risk = $2,190.

Maximum Profit = $810.

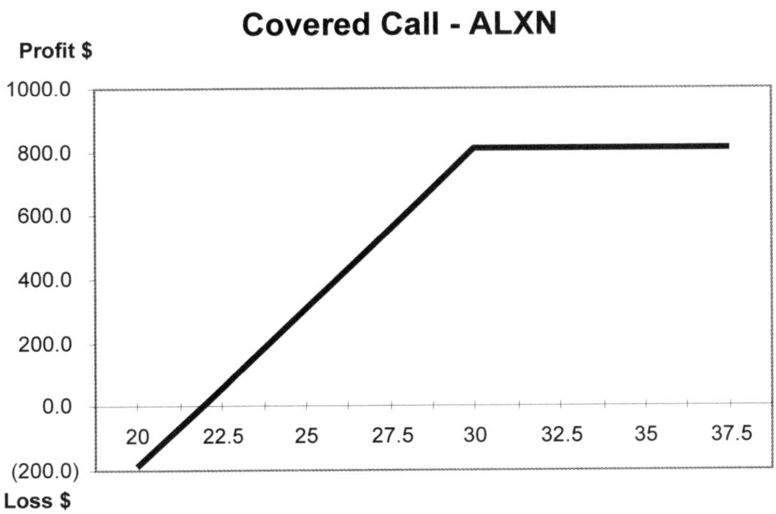

---

[2] PowerOptions 02 February 2009 < http://www.poweropt.com/cchelp.asp>

Breakeven point: strike price – premium received.

Maximum profit: where stock settles at or above strike price.

Loss increases as stock falls.

Advantages of selling covered calls

The seller receives the premium for the calls sold on the date of transaction. This process can be repeated as the calls expire, potentially compounding gains.

The seller can close the position by buying the call option back prior to the expiration date, if desired.

Disadvantages of selling covered calls

If the price rises above the strike price, the seller's profit would be limited

In most instances, the seller cannot sell the stock without buying the option back first. If the stock was sold and the option remained open, the result would be a Naked Call. Most brokerages have strict limitations on Naked Calls.

Chapter 9

Stop Loss orders

A stop loss is an accepted and commonly used term, but it is actually incorrect.

The correct term is "stop order". However, the two terms are used interchangeably. It is however, an order to buy or sell a specific security if the market price for that security reaches a designated price. It is used to preserve profit or minimize loss in stock trading. You can use this order either to buy or to sell a security when the price goes to the designated price.

There are two main types of stop orders:

1. Stop Limit Order

A stop limit order means that a limit order is entered to buy or sell a security if it reaches a designated price. As it is a limit order, it is not guaranteed to be executed.

For example, if an investor owns 500 shares of ABC Corporation at a cost of $25.00 and wants to limit the risk to only $1,500.00, the investor may choose to enter a stop limit order at $22.00. That means that if the market price of ABC were to go to $22.00, a sell order with a limit price of $22.00 would be triggered. The sell order has a required price of $22.00 or greater, meaning, it will not be executed if the stock were to continue to trade lower. Resulting in the investor still being at risk, and the amount at risk can be significantly more than the $1,500.00 he intended.

2. Stop Order (also known as a Stop Market Order)

Without the designation of a limit price, a stop order is executed is executed at the market price, once it is triggered. Simply put, if the price of the stock goes to a designated price, the stop order becomes a market order and is immediately executed.

For example, if an investor owns 500 shares of ABC Corporation at a cost of $25.00 per share, and again decides to limit risk to $1,500.00, he may choose to [enter stop order (no limit price designated) at $22.00. This means that if ABC declined to $22.00 or lower, the shares are immediately sold at the then current market price.

The downfall of stop orders is that sometimes stocks can "gap" up or down. That means that the stock closes at a price one day, and opens the following morning a much higher or lower price. As outlined above, the investor has a stop order in at $22.00. If ABC Corporation closed trading on Monday at $23.50, and made a negative news announcement after the close, such as bad earnings, the stock may open Tuesday at $15.00. This would result in the immediate execution of the sell stop (market) and the stop limit order would not be executed. As result in each example, the investor has risked far more than the $1,500.00 they intended to risk.

In the case of a sell stop (either market or limit); the order would be triggered if the market price of the security was at or below the designated stop price. In the case of a buy stop (either market or limit); it would be triggered at or above the designated stop price.

Usage of a stop loss order means the investor need not track price movements of the underlying stock all the time. However, it is sometimes disadvantageous for the investors as the order to buy or sell will be executed if the price touches the stop price. As a result, short term swings in price that cause stop orders to be executed in your account, can have a lasting impact on your portfolio. This is precisely the reason why many investors would choose to purchase a put, rather enter a sell stop on a long position, and purchase a call rather enter a buy stop on a short position.

In spite of putting stop losses in place, some investors choose to exit before stop orders are executed. There are three common reasons for this:

- Technical changes; many traders enter into trade based on their analysis. When they base their decisions on their technical analysis, they may not wish to maintain a position if an unexpected change occurs in the technical pattern. As a result, a trader may choose to exit the trade as they become neutral or reverse their opinion.

- Geopolitical factors; major external factors including political changes sometimes affect markets. They have wide-reaching effects on stock prices.
- Time factor; when traders a trade for a short term gains, the price may or may not hit the technical signals, resulting in some traders elected to close positions.

Here are some variations of stop orders.

1. Trailing Stop Limit

This works in the same manner as the stop limit, but the stop limit price would increase as the stock does. The stop limit price here rises by the same amount the stock does, but remains unchanged when there is fall in the stock price. A limit order will be submitted at the price given when order price gets triggered. All other aspects are identical to stop limit orders.

4. Trailing Stop

Just like a trailing stop limit is similar to a stop limit, so is a trailing stop order similar to a stop order. The stop price here will be fixed at a price below its market price. The stop price goes up with increase in the market price and if the stock price decreases, the stop price remains unchanged.

It is important to remember that not all brokerages provide the ability to enter trailing stop and trailing stop limit orders. If the brokerage does not offer this service as an automatic occurrence, it can be done manually by changing the stop price yourself on a regular basis.

Chapter 10

Beginning to Trade

Entering and Exiting Option Trades

As the option trading depends on the value of the underlying asset, a small change in the option price would give greater results on returns. The bid is the highest price a trader is willing to pay to buy an option whereas the ask price is the lowest price a trader is willing to accept to sell an option. The ask price is almost always higher than the bid price. The best (highest) bid and the best (lowest) offer combine for what is called the inside bid and ask or inside market. The difference between these two is called the "bid-ask spread", or spread for short. This should not be confused with a spread option strategy as they are two separate things. The spread will be narrow for most liquid assets and will be wider for illiquid assets. In particularly volatile markets, the bid ask spread tends to wider than in less volatile markets.

When to enter a trade

An opening transaction can be made with a market order or with a limit order. When dealing in options, it is generally not recommended to use market orders, as they tend to increase the immediate volatility resulting in executions that differ significantly from the original inside market.

Typically, it is best to utilize limit orders when entering option trades. However, it is important to make sure your limit price is reasonable in light of the inside market. An investor may choose to do what is known as "split the spread". This means they enter their limit price between the best bid and best ask. That would make their order the best bid or ask, depending on whether the trade is a buy or sell order. There is no guarantee that limit orders will get filled because there is no guarantee that the market will demand the limit price. The only order that is absolutely guaranteed execution is a market order.

Let me try to explain with the following examples.

Example – 1

Bid price and ask price of an option are $1.70 – $1.75. The spread is very tight here. Assuming that it is highly liquid stock, a limit order can be placed at $1.75 to get the order filled, as long as your buy order is not for more contracts then are available at the offer price.

Example – 2

Bid and ask prices of an option are $1.70 and 2.10. The spread here is tight with $0.40 which gives opportunity for "negotiation". You can enter into the trade by placing a limit order at $1.90, splitting the spread.

Example – 3

Bid and ask prices of an option are $5.20 and $5.50, respectively. The spread here is $0.40 which indicates scope for negotiation. In this instance, a seller of an option may to choose to enter a limit order at $5.40, whereas a seller may choose $5.30 as the limit price.

When entering a trade, it is important to be realistic with your limit order or you will likely not be executed. A seller of an option always wants to get the most they can, and a buyer wants to pay the least. Let us not forget that a difference in price of $0.10 equals a difference in trade value of $10.00 per contract! Of course if you are entering a trade with one hundred contracts, that can add up to a significant cost difference. In most instances, trades that only involve only a handful of contracts are dramatically affected by that difference of $0.10. While it important to remain disciplined and not overpay, if you are truly confident about the strategy you are implementing, it may be prudent in certain instances to increase your limit price in order preserve you opportunity in the option strategy.

Exiting from a trade

One can exit a trade by placing a market order or with a limit order. One can also use other alternatives, such as placing a stop loss order or a stop limit order. A long option can be sold and a stop loss order can be placed to exit.

Example – 1

Bid price and ask prices of an option are $1.70 and 1.75. Assuming the number of contracts is not greater than number of contracts to be bought at the bid price, a sell limit order would be filled if it is entered at $1.70.

Example – 2

Bid price and ask prices of an option are $1.70 and 2.10. One can split the spread, and place the order at $1.90 in an effort to get the order filled in neutral trading conditions. While execution is not guaranteed, it is likely to be executed if entered between the inside bid and ask.

Example – 3

Bid and ask prices of an option are $5.20 and $5.50. The spread here is $0.40 which indicates scope for negotiation. If a buy limit order were executed at $5.40, the investor may have overpaid. It would be smart to enter a buy limit order at $5.30, making it the inside bid. If the $5.30 limit is not executed after some time, it may be prudent to increase to $5.40. It is important to avoid "chasing prices". Not every trade will be executed at the price you need. You must be disciplined.

In the case of selling options, an order to sell options will be activated when it trades at trigger price or lower; or when the ask price is equal or less than trigger price. It becomes a market order to sell once it is activated. It is preferred to use this order under extreme conditions to avoid losses. Not all brokerages will offer the ability to enter orders such as this on options. You must ensure that the brokerage you select provides that service.

Example

You have a long call that is currently trading at $3.50. A sell limit order of $3.00 can be placed to stop or minimize the loss with a trigger price of $3.20. If the ask price drops down to $3.10 and the bid price to 2.90, the limit order to sell at $3.00 will be activated, however, the order may not get filled as the bid price is lower than the limit price. With proper forecasting and anticipation the order could have been filled if trigger price is set at $3.20 and bid price at $3.00.

Anxiety of getting assigned

An option cannot be assigned if the short option price is out-of-the-money.

Example

Let us assume that the stock price of ABC in December is $43 and you are short a December 45 call. No one would exercise the calls to buy at $45 as the shares can be purchased in the open market at $43 per share. Also, if you were short a December 40 put, that also would not be executed as the stock can be sold for $43 in the open market

An option is unlikely to be assigned early if there is sufficient time value included in the option premium.

Example

Assume that the stock price of ABC stock is $23.50 and you own a December 22.50 call that has a bid of $1.50. You are unlikely to exercise the option if the time value [1.50 – (23.50-22.50)] is included in the option price. It would be better if you buy stock in the open market at $23.50 and sell your call for $1.50. You can save $0.50 by giving up opportunity to collect $1.50 per share.

An early assignment is possible when the expiration date approaches closer and when time value begins disappearing quickly.

Example

The price of ABC stock is $24.50 during second week of December and you have a December 25 put whose bid price is $0.60. The time value here is $0.10 [0.60-(25-24.50)]. This situation gives opportunity for early assignment.

Ready to trade?

Once you have carefully read about and practiced the different strategies, and you are convinced you have the knowledge and self-discipline to trade options, you may carefully begin to do so. Be careful that any time you place an order that involves a combination of options; you must place the order as a net result of credit or debit. Never ever place an order for one side of the option hoping to fill the other side later. It is quite likely; you may not be able to fill the other side of the option after one side has been filled.

It cannot be stressed enough that you must concentrate on preserving your capital. Do not be greedy, or to aggressive. Use the strategies whereby if the stock does the opposite of what you expected, you do not end up losing more than you can handle. Once you begin losing your capital, you will have to make that much more just to break even.

It is OK if you do not make any money, but you do not lose your capital.

Do not forget, it takes the right strategies combined with the self-discipline to make money on a consistent basis.

Brokers and commissions

Friends who are trading stocks or options may recommend the names of brokerages. Market surveys will further help you in identifying the right brokers.

Different brokers charge different fees per different services, particularly in options. Several levels of commission rates exist in the system. A full service broker may charge a low rate per option contract and then charge additional fee per order. The broker here provides step-by-step guidance to the customer. He provides advice on purchase of shares and options and provides full support to customers. This is useful for those who are new to options trading and want to get advice from professionals.

A discount broker will not give you advice on the investment, nor help with detailed research, but may offer direct access trading. The broker carries out transactions as per the instructions of the customers. They charge a lower rate for trading. This arrangement is for those who have experience in options trading and need no help with their trading. The trading platform is highly sophisticated and has links with all exchanges. One can enter and exit from the trade with click of a button. The cost of trading will be much less with electronic trading. It is advisable to check around with many brokers, both full-service and discount, before you settle on which brokerage to select.

Factors to be considered when selecting the right broker:

- Check for availability of good brokers.
- Look for responsiveness of brokers to overcome an investor's limitations and satisfy their needs.
- Check honesty and trustworthiness of the brokers.
- Collect the names of past customers and try to learn how broker has performed overall.
- Know the system of recommendations generally offered by the brokers.
- Experience, financial stability and track record of the broker.
- Look for conveniences like ease of access in quotes, account information, analysis tools, types of orders that can be entered, etc.
- Look for an order entry and execution mechanism of transactions.
- Seek information about the reliability of hardware and software used by the brokers.
- Check if the broker has any hidden fees.
- Check if the broker is already a public company.
- Know the initial deposit requirement to open an account.

- Check the performance of website (proneness to errors, speed during peek hours etc.).

As our best strategies are the ones which involve selling the options rather than buying options, it is extremely important that you find a broker who is experienced in selling options. It is unfortunate that it is not an easy task, as most brokers are not trained in these strategies.

If you are not able to find a suitable broker, send us an e mail through our website www.BillionaireBestSellers.com. Explain us your needs. We will try to give you a reference depending upon your needs.

Chapter 11

Web sites and magazines

The lists of websites and publications are not designed to be all encompassing, nor is it an endorsement of the information, products or services offered. It meant simply to provide an avenue for you to obtain additional information, enabling you to do your own research.

Important Websites

www.cboe.com—Chicago Board Options Exchange founded in 1973 and it is the largest options trading exchange.

www.optionsexpress.com—one of the leading brokerage firms providing online brokerage services.

www.cme.com—world's largest and most diverse financial exchange

www.phlx.com—Philadelphia Stock Exchange

www.chicagostockex.com—Chicago Stock Exchange

www.amex.com—American Stock Exchange

www.pacificex.com—Pacific Stock Exchange, Inc

www.cincinnatistock.com—The Cincinnati Stock Exchange

www.iseoptions.com—International Securities Exchange

www.nyse.com—New York Stock Exchange

www.nasdaq.com—NASDAQ Stock Market

www.bostonstock.com—Boston Stock Exchange, Inc

www.nymex.com—New York Mercantile Exchange

Important publications

- OptionVue Newsletter, edited by Jim Graham and Steve Lentz (www.optionvueresearch.com)
- The Option Adviser, edited by Bernie Schaffer (www.schaeffersresearch.com)
- Daily Option Strategist, edited by Larry McMillan (www.optionstrategist.com)
- BigTrends.com Newsletter, edited by Price Headley (www.bigtrends.com)
- SFO Magazine (www.sfomag.com)
- Active Trader Magazine (www.activetradermag.com)

Important tools

- www.optionvue.com—provides option analysis software, other web-based tools and advisory services to individual and professional traders
- www.888options.com—a non-profit association engaged in educating investors about the risks and benefits of exchanged traded equity options.
- www.tradestation.com—Online Trading Platform
- www.dtniq.com—Online Quote Service
- www.alphatrade.com—Online Quote Service
- www.cqg.com—Provider of Trading Software
- www.equis.com—Online Quote and Research Service
- www.barchart.com—Online Research Service
- www.ivolatility.com—Online Research and Analysis
- www.rpsw.com—Software Provider

- www.option-chart.com—Allows You to Compute Profit/Loss on Potential Trades, Depending on the Price of the Underlying
- www.otrader.com.au—Online Trading Position Manager

- www.mindxpansion.com—Software Provider
- www.optionstar.com—Provider of Option Analysis Software
- www.quotein.com—Provider of Software that Converts Market Data into a Spreadsheet
- www.fintools.com—Provider of Financial Software and Templates
- www.spooztoolz.com—Online Trading Platform
- www.poweropt.com—Online Research Tool
- www.stockfetcher.com—Stock Screening and Analysis
- www.trade-ideas.com—Real Time Stock Alert Scanner
- www.marketscreen.com—Security Screening, Research and Analysis
- www.elitetrader.com—Online Community and Forum For Traders
- www.optionstrategist.com—Options Trading Resources, Advice and Commentary
- www.optionetics.com—Investment Education Resource
- www.stockcharts.com—Online Research Service
- www.bigcharts.com—Online Research Service
- www.futuresmag.com—Derivatives Periodical
- www.TDAmeritrade.com—Online Trading Platform
- www.scottrade.com—Online Trading Platform
- www.schwab.com—Online Trading Platform

Glossary

American Exercise—the ability to exercise an option at any time prior to expiration

Ask Price—the price at which a writer is willing to sell an option or stock

Assigned—notification that an option which a seller is short has been exercised, and the writer must complete their obligation under the terms of the option contract

At the Money—a term illustrating that the strike price of the option in question is approximately equal to the current market price

Bearish—a sentiment where an individual feels a stock, index, or the market will have a downward trend

Bid Price—the price which a purchaser is willing to pay to buy an option or stock

Broker—an individual or organization that executes transaction on behalf of another

Bullish—a sentiment where an individual feels a stock, index, or the market will have an upward trend

Call—an option contract where the holder, or buyer, has the right to purchase a specific stock, at a specific price, during a specific time, regardless of the then current market price

Collar—when the underlying stock is owned, combined with a long out of the money put, and a short out of the money call

Commission—a fee paid to a broker to execute a transaction on behalf of an investor

Credit Spread—an option strategy involving one long and one short option contract, and the premium paid for the long option is less than then premium received for the short option

Debit Spread—an option strategy involving one long and one short option contract, and the premium paid for the long option is greater than the premium received for the short option

European Exercise—the ability to exercise an option only at its expiration

Execution—the price at which a transaction occurs

Exercise—the act of invoking the rights given to the holder of an option

Expiration Date—the date where the rights associated with an option are no longer valid, and the option may no longer be exercised

Hedge—the act of attempting to minimize risk by supplementing an investment position, such as with a married put

In the Money—a term illustrating that the strike price of the option in question is greater than the current market price in the case of puts, and lower than the current market price in the case of calls

Intrinsic Value—the portion of the option premium that is not time value, it represents the inherent market value if exercised

Leverage—an investment tool that magnifies both risk and potential reward

Liquidity—a measure of the ability to convert an asset to cash without causing a significant impact on the market price of the asset

Long—a term illustrating that asset is owned

Loss—when a position is closed, and it is worth less than when it was opened

Margin Requirement—the amount of funds required by the broker to maintain an open position

Married—a term symbolizing that one position is tied to another, such as when one is long the underlying and simultaneously long a protective put, it is said to be a married put

Naked—a term illustrating a stand alone option, if an individual sells a call and does not own the underlying, it is said to be a naked call

Neutral—when sentiment is neither bullish nor bearish

Open Interest—a measure of the total number of option contracts in a series presently in an open position

Option—the right to buy or sell a specific stock, at a specific price, during a specific time, regardless of the then current market price

Option Chain—a manner of quoting prices for the available options for a specific security

Options Clearing Corporation (OCC)—the organization that clears options trades, it is equally owned by its member exchanges

Options Exchange—an organization that enables transactions, either physical or electronic, in options

Out of the Money—a term illustrating that the strike price of the option in question is greater than the current market price in the case of calls, and lower than the current market price in the case of puts

Premium—in the case of a buyer it is the price paid to purchase an option contract, in the case of a seller it is the price received for selling the option

Profit—when a position is closed, and it is worth more than when it was opened

Put—an option contract where the holder, or buyer, has the right to sell a specific stock, at a specific price, during a specific time, regardless of the then current market price

Quote—the price of an option or stock

Risk—the potential for loss

Settlement Date—the date, by which a transaction must be paid for, typically it is one business day for options, and three business days for stocks

Short—the act of selling a security which is not presently owned

Stock—a share of ownership interest in a corporation

Stop Limit Order—a limit order entered electronically once the market value of a security reaches a certain price

Stop Loss Order (Stop Order)—a market order entered electronically once the market value of a security reaches a certain price

Straddle—simultaneously purchasing or selling an at the money put and call on the same security, with the same expiration and same strike

Strangle—simultaneously purchasing or selling an out of the money put and call on the same security, with the same expiration and same strike

Strategy—a calculated plan in order to attain a goal

Strike Price—the pre-designated price at which a security will change hands if an option is exercised

Time Decay—the depreciation of an option as it nears expiration

Time Value—the portion of an option premium that is paid for the amount of time remaining until expiration of the option

Underlying Asset—the security on which the option is based

Volatility—a measure of the price fluctuation of an asset

Volume—the number of contracts of options, or shares of stock, that change hands during a trading day

Warrant—the contractual ability to buy shares of a corporation, similar to an option, but written by the corporation and usually the strike price is higher than the current market price when it is written

Write—to sell an option contract